The Clay-Pot Cookbook

The Clay-Pot Cookbook

A New Way of Cooking

IN AN

Ancient Pot

───────

Georgia MacLeod Sales

AND

Grover Sales

FOREWORD BY HERBERT GOLD

ILLUSTRATIONS BY DAVID LANCE GOINES

Atheneum   New York

1978

Library of Congress catalog card number: 74-81233
ISBN 0-689-70547-6
Published simultaneously in Canada by McClelland and Stewart Ltd.
Manufactured by The Murray Printing Company,
Forge Village, Massachusetts
Designed by Kathleen Carey

TO

Leah Bloom

AND

Barbara Thomas

Contents

Foreword

BY HERBERT GOLD

M Y own skill in cooking has consisted mainly of marrying people who know how. Once I was asked to contribute my personal recipe to *The Artists' and Writers' Cookbook* and could only come up with:

PRUNES IN WHITE SAUCE
Soak prunes in water.
Pour milk over.

It's evident that Georgia and Grover Sales have made a great discovery. I have eaten whereof I speak. I thought Etruscan clay cooking was merely delicious and healthful, now I discover that it is also economical. That spoils nothing. Another perfection does no harm.

Bless them. Whether or not they start an Etruscan revival, they are busy with their good deeds in the kitchen. I hope to be invited soon again.

P.S. For the prunes in white sauce, it helps to use boiling water. Also to seal in a Mason jar. Probably the ancient Etruscans had a better way.

Cooking with Wet Clay:
Hows and Whys, Dos and Don'ts

WHAT'S THE DIFFERENCE?

Cooking with terra-cotta wet clay, dating back to the ancient Etruscans, is *not* to be confused with ordinary clay-casserole cooking.

The crucial difference is that the unglazed terra-cotta pot —both top and bottom—is totally immersed in water for at least 10 minutes before cooking. Then, wet-clay cooking is self-basting, and produces its own natural sauces. And the diet-conscious can cook without fat while preserving all the food value and flavor.

Most clay casserole pots are glazed, either on the outside, inside, or both. You probably have such pots in your kitchen, but these "dry" cookers will not give you the unique results of the Etruscan wet-pot.

What you are looking for is an *unglazed* pot of very porous, highly fired clay. Many pots of this type are made in Germany by Romertopf, and come in a useful variety of sizes. An excellent small "poulet form" is imported from France.

Once sold on this method of cooking, you will want to own pots in about three sizes. The larger models, like the Romertopf No. 113, are handy for serving complete dinners for a party of six, with all the meat and vegetables cooked together. You may also want to cook two different dishes at once, say, a turkey in the large pot and eggplant with tomatoes and cheese, perhaps, in a smaller pot.

WHAT ELSE WILL YOU NEED?

Get a sturdy pair of asbestos barbecue gloves for handling the hot pot.

Get a reliable oven thermometer. Temperature controls on many older ovens are often off as much as 40 degrees. You'll get more consistent results for "time and temperature" cooking if you rely on a good mercury thermometer rather than the dial indicator on your range.

Use a meat thermometer, the dial kind that can fit inside the wet-pot. Those with a sliding pointer are easier to read. Since cooking time is affected by the size of the pot and the amount of food it contains, the meat thermometer is sometimes your best guide. Always remove the pot from the oven when the thermometer is *almost* up to temperature; don't wait until it's right on the pointer or you'll overcook.

RULES OF WET-CLAY COOKING

1. Always submerge the top and bottom of the pot in water for at least 10 to 15 minutes prior to cooking.

2. Place the filled and "watered" pot in a *cold* oven. *Don't preheat!* This slow bringing up to temperature is essential to get the most out of your pot.

3. Place the pot near the center of the oven.

4. Use a very high temperature—450 to 480 degrees.

5. About 10 minutes before the end of cooking time, remove the pot from the oven and pour the liquid into a pan for making the sauce. For additional browning or "crisping" of meat or fowl, replace the pot in the oven with the top off for the final 10 minutes of cooking.

6. Remember: The larger the pot and the more food it contains, the longer the cooking time.

7. *Trim off as much fat as you can before cooking.* Even if you're not on a diet, you won't want all that fat in your sauces. To keep the fatless meat from getting too dry, add a little liquid to the pot, preferably wine. Since the alcohol in the wine is consumed while cooking, weight watchers need not worry. Use oil sparingly, or better, substitute butter for oil. Some Oriental recipes call for sesame oil, but only in small amounts.

8. Use plenty of salt in the pot, *except* when soy sauce is called for, or in cooking corned beef, which has already been marinated in brine. The amounts of salt called for in our recipes may seem excessive—they are not. This type of cooking requires unusual amounts of salt.

THICKENING THE SAUCES, AND THE USES OF ARROWROOT

Many of the recipes in this book call for *arrowroot* to thicken the liquid produced by cooking in a water-soaked clay pot.

If you are used to thickening sauces with flour or cornstarch, we suggest you switch to arrowroot, which is available in the spice department of any grocery.

The amount of arrowroot given in any recipe is only an approximation, depending on the amount of liquid produced in the clay pot, and most of all, your own taste for a thick or a thin sauce. A bit of experimentation will determine the amount of arrowroot you prefer.

Dissolve the approximate amount of arrowroot (about 1 to 1½ teaspoons) in a little hot water—or wine if you prefer.

Pour the liquid from the clay pot into a saucepan, bring to a boil and add the arrowroot solution a little at a time, stirring constantly, until the sauce is thickened to your taste.

CARE, CLEANING, AND REPAIR OF THE WET-CLAY POT

1. Clean the pot with scalding hot water and a stiff brush *only; never* use soaps or detergents. They will clog the pores and impart a soapy taste to your cooking. Stubborn crusts are easily removed with very coarse stainless steel wool "ribbons," *unsoaped* of course.

2. Never store the pot with the lid in cooking position, but turn the lid upside down in the pot. Allowing air to circulate keeps the pot from turning rancid.

3. Never place a hot pot on a cold or wet surface, or it will crack. Place it on a towel or a wooden chopping block.

4. Before you use a new pot for the first time, remove the clay dust by scrubbing with hot water and a stiff brush. It helps to "age" a new pot by soaking it in water and then "firing" the wet, empty pot in a hot oven. This method is also handy for cleaning an old pot after repeated use.

5. Never stack other dishes or utensils on top of the pot. This will lead to cracks and breakage.

6. No need to throw out a cracked pot; even large fissures can be easily mended. Elmer's two-part epoxy glue is splendid for this purpose, and will withstand high oven temperatures. Before mending, dry the pot thoroughly in a hot oven and allow to cool, but apply the epoxy while the pot is still warm to the touch. It will dry diamond-hard in a few hours if placed in a warm oven, about 100 degrees.

Authors' Preface

ON HOW A MODEST CLAY POT—and a good woman—converted a bachelor from the delights of dining out to the joy of home cooking:

Our first year together, Georgia kept saying "I can't understand why you never learned to cook. If you had your way, there'd be some wild new dish every night—hippopotamus lips under glass, kumquats jubilee. You love music, wine, the theater—it all goes together. How come you never cooked for yourself?"

As a longtime bachelor, the notion of cooking, even breakfast bacon and eggs, rarely intrigued me once I happened upon the joys of dining out. In the late Thirties I moved to Boston from my native Louisville, whose cuisine, aside from the superb aged beef of the Bourbon Stockyards, was an endless round of grits, molasses, and biscuits, and for

Sunday dinner a boiled chicken, canned green peas, and mashed potatoes. Don't ever let anyone con you about "good old Southern home cooking"; except for New Orleans, which is more French-Creole than South, it's a laughable myth. My flight from Dixie may have been due to a subliminal urge to get away from that cooking. Also, there was little "live" jazz in Kentucky, and I had gone bug-eyed out of my mind over Benny Goodman.

My first week in Boston, I gravitated toward the local jazz crowd, all much older and wiser. They taught me that good food and wine go with music you love. After a Duke Ellington dance date, they took me to my first Chinese restaurant, Ruby Foo's near Symphony Hall, where a dozen of us shared scores of dishes. I was hooked. Next week they introduced me to the Old Union Oyster House, wallowing in soft-shell crab, fried clams, and huge-clawed lobsters. I then determined to erase the memory of a deprived culinary past by tasting everything God meant us to.

Then came the war (what Lenny Bruce called "the *good* War—the War Against Hitler"). Four years of army *haute cuisine:* unmentionable guck from massive kitchens that never saw wine, garlic, or olive oil. Daily I fantasized myself as a jaded voluptuary gorging on squab with wild rice under glass, washed down with a slightly chilled Auslese. I tortured myself reading of Ludwig Bemelmans' gustatory bouts in Parisian hotels.

The closest I ever came to civilized dining during the four terrible army years was in Dibrugarh, a Himalayan foothill town in Assam. Fleeing from an army mess (appropriate name) of uncommon squalor even by army standards, I flirted with a general court-martial nearly every night, AWOL-ing it to Kwan Yin's, a remote village restaurant run by twelve Chinese brothers. All the money saved for postwar college was lavished on steamed duck smothered in crisp hot greens, suckling pig with spiced baked apples encrusted in delicate cinnamon pastry, doused in an orange and brandy sauce. "When I get out of Uncle Whiskers," I thought, "it'll be this way every night."

The education guiltily squandered at Kwan Yin's was paid for by the G.I. Bill at a small college in Portland, Oregon. The fare at the common dining hall was so debased that I took to bringing a box of condiments to the table. The campus nutritionist warned me: "You're going to eat away the lining of your innards with all those hot spices," following a lunch-eon of boiled whitefish, watery cauliflower, macaroni salad. and a dollop of lemon Jell-O for exotic color. The govern-ment's forty-eight dollars a month didn't allow for much dining out—especially in Portland, once described by Herb Caen as "a town where, if you go into a restaurant and order wine, they think you're a fruit."

So dining out stayed a dream deferred until I moved to San Francisco in the late Forties, when the City still boasted of countless nontourist down-home eateries—Chinese, German, French, Greek, and mainly Italian family-style, with groan-ing seven-course spreads including a carafe of gusty Gri-gnolino and dark, pungent espresso with a twist of lemon peel—all for little more than the price of a first-run movie, in those days about $1.25. With this kind of dining out, who needed to cook?

Then restaurant prices began their Korean War climb, and

the hunt for honest out-of-the-way havens was on. Once you found one, so did Herb Caen (in San Francisco, everybody reads him). Within weeks the owners of a once-convivial unknown spot would redecorate, expand, boost the prices, water the wine, skimp on the food. I started to cook, with less than Cordon Bleu results.

Then I met Georgia, who asked me why I didn't cook. To all the foregoing I could only add, "Why should I cook when you do it so well? It would be *inhibiting* to cook with you around." Georgia's a studying cook with an awesome library of James Beard, Louis deGouy and ten years' back issues of *Gourmet* that don't just sit there, she *reads* them. Couldn't see struggling my way through a *sauce béarnaise* with a jewel like Georgia in the kitchen.

Christmas shopping changed all this. I was seeking some kitchen marvel Georgia might not own and came across this rough-hewn, unglazed terra-cotta pot. "I never used one," said the clerk, "but one customer tells me it makes the juiciest chicken she ever tasted."

Wherefore, I wondered, is this different from all other pots? A pamphlet explained that, unlike the usual glazed casseroles, this pot, both top and bottom, was totally submerged in water for 10 minutes before cooking. The highly fired porous clay soaked up water like a sponge. When baked at high temperatures, 450 to 480 degrees, the steam commingled with the natural juices of the pot's contents to penetrate the innermost fibers of meats, fish, and vegetables. Weight watchers could cook without fat, oil, or butter. Fowl and beef cooked in this way had a unique texture, different from boiling, roasting, pressure cooking, rotisserie or microwave.

They said it did wonders for seafood and corn on the cob. Best of all, the wet-clay pot manufactured its own sauce. When archeologists unearthed ancient Etruscan cities, this was the sort of cookware they found.

Intrigued, I bore my first unglazed pot home to Georgia. Having lived through my passions for photography and hi-fi with *Le Sacre du Printemps* at concert hall levels, she viewed my new enthusiasm with tolerant disdain.

"Honey—don't we have *enough* pots around here?"

"But this is different—you soak the pot in water . . ."

"I know. You told me four times."

"But you always *said* I should cook. I want to try it."

That night I cooked my first chicken, laboring over the beast like some sweaty midwife, massaging her with salt and pepper, painting her with a brilliant mixture of paprika, oil, crushed garlic, and minced fresh rosemary. I added little white onions, chopped parsley, tiny new potatoes, carrots, mushrooms, grated Monterey Jack and white wine. Popping the water-soaked pot into a cold oven, I turned the thermostat to 480 degrees—and waited.

Soon the most delectable odor filled the house. Georgia's youngest, Grant, came bounding in from school: "What's for dinner? Smelled it all the way down the block!"

Ninety minutes later I grabbed asbestos gloves, removed the pot, opened the lid and poured the bubbling orange sauce into a hot pan. Georgia showed me how to thicken it with arrowroot. It was a smash. The bird had a plump, running-over succulence, the skin was golden brown, the carrots could have doubled as dessert. Even the mundane little new potatoes took on an exotic cast. But it was the sauce that did it. The juices that came pouring out of that pot—an intoxicating fusion of bird, wine, herbs, and roots—was something to serve at Maxim's in a Cellini bowl. Georgia became rhapsodic: "You were right! It is different—and absolutely marvelous!"

We cooked with the wet-clay pot every night, always experimenting and making new discoveries. Cheap, tough cuts of beef came out buttery tender as filet. Boneless rolled shoulder of lamb, one of the least costly of meats, was made to order for the pot. A miniature New England clambake with steaming shellfish, fresh corn, and potatoes lent itself to endless variations. And what happened to pork loin roast with little green apples was something of a miracle.

We bought two larger size pots to accommodate dinner guests who begged for seconds, gasping between gulps, "Grover—when did *you* learn to cook?"

Soon I was cooking every night—me, the confirmed eater-outer. It was so easy. No books to read, no mountains of pans to juggle. Just half an hour to fill the watered pot, stash it in the oven, walk the dogs, linger over a six-o'clock vermouth, and it was ready to serve from the pot.

Georgia adapted twenty years of creative cooking and recipe hunting to the new method, tempering my wilder caprices with gentle restraint: "I really don't think it's a good idea to mix green chartreuse in with the shallots." Some of my impulses she resisted with surprising vigor; it took six months to get her to try corned beef: "You have to *simmer* it gently for hours, or it'll be tough. Everything won't work in the pot and corned beef happens to be one of them." When the corned beef turned out great after two hours, Georgia was sold. She even suggested baking, inspired by Julian Street's essay on French bread: "There must be steam in the oven. . . . The following recipe will produce as good a loaf as it is possible to make in the ordinary American household range, with heat coming not evenly from all sides but from the bottom only." Of course it made perfect sense. The wet-clay pot was a natural French oven that turned out magnificent bread, moist, yet firm, plump and gorgeously browned. We started making everything in the pot but ice cream.

Writing a cookbook seemed as remote to me as dashing off an oratorio in the style of Handel, until we combed bookstores for new recipes—only to find a remarkable lack of guides to ancient Etruscan cooking. Aside from Romertopf's helpful though brief booklet, *Cook in Clay,* there was little in print.

Our gourmet friends proved no help. They had never even heard of this style of cooking. One couple gifted with a Romertopf pot for Christmas never took it out of the box: "We didn't know what to do with it." Georgia and I fed them our San Francisco clambake and they've cooked this way ever since. Friends began phoning for recipes. Georgia started nudging: "You're a writer, I'm a cook. When do we start?"

So this happy discovery of an experienced cook and an absolute beginner was something we wanted to share with others, whether master chefs like Georgia, or fumbling amateurs like me.

GROVER SALES

Chicken, Duck & Game

ROAST CHICKEN WITH BROWN RICE STUFFING

(SERVES 4 TO 6)

If asked to name the most successful dish we ever cooked in the Etruscan clay pot, this would be it. More than any other recipe, this juicy and succulent chicken with the unequaled stuffing and sauce made our dinner guest go out and buy a pot the next day.

For a table of six, we cook *two* roasting chickens in the large turkey-size pot. We found *brown* rice gives the stuffing a lustier, stick-to-the-ribs taste and texture, and we get good results with Uncle Ben's. Remember: A larger pot and the stuffing both add cooking time.

> 1 *roasting chicken* (*4 to 5 pounds*)
> ¾ *cup sherry*
> 1¾ *cups chicken stock*
> 1 *cup raw brown rice*
> 2 *tablespoons butter*
> *Arrowroot*

STUFFING:
> ⅓ *cup pine nuts*
> ⅓ *cup dried currants*
> 3 *chicken livers, diced*

6 *large shallots, chopped fine*

1 *small onion, diced*

1 *teaspoon dried sage (or 8 chopped leaves of fresh sage)*

¼ *teaspoon dried rosemary (or ½ teaspoon fresh chopped rosemary)*

2 *tablespoons fresh chopped parsley*

2 *teaspoons salt*

¼ *teaspoon fresh ground pepper*

Marinate whole roasting chicken in ½ cup sherry for 3 to 4 hours. Turn often.

Bring chicken stock to boil in saucepan, add rice and butter; cover and simmer for 20 minutes. (The rice will not be done.)

Presoak pot, top and bottom, in water for 15 minutes.

In large mixing bowl, combine the stuffing.

Add the rice and whatever liquid is not absorbed, and ¼ cup sherry.

Remove chicken from marinade. Rub the insides lightly with salt. Stuff with the dressing, sew up the opening, and truss the chicken.

Rub outside of bird with butter and lightly salt.

Place chicken in presoaked pot and add remaining sherry marinade.

Cover and place pot in cold oven.

Set temperature to 480 degrees.

Cook 80 minutes.

Remove from oven and test for doneness by wiggling a leg— if it moves freely in its socket, it's almost done.

Baste chicken and return to oven *without* the lid to brown

for about 10 minutes. Watch carefully and baste frequently.

Pour sauce into heated pan, adjust seasoning if necessary, bring to a boil and thicken with arrowroot. Serve the sauce in a side dish.

CHICKEN WITH KIDNEYS AND SOUR CREAM
(SERVES 4)

This variation turns out the chicken surprise of the year, with lamb kidneys, sour cream, and herbs bringing out all kinds of unsuspected charms in the bird.

> *1 whole chicken (3 pounds)*
> *Salt*
> *Pepper*
> *3 tablespoons olive oil*
> *1 tablespoon paprika*
> *2 small cloves garlic, crushed*
> *1 teaspoon fresh thyme (or ½ teaspoon dried)*
> *1 teaspoon fresh sage (or ½ teaspoon dried)*
> *4 lamb kidneys*
> *10 large mushrooms, sliced*
> *Butter*
> *½ pint sour cream*
> *½ cup white wine*
> *Arrowroot*

Presoak pot, top and bottom, in water for 15 minutes.

Wash chicken inside and out under cold running water.

Rub inside of chicken with salt and pepper.

Paint chicken inside and out with mixture of olive oil, paprika, crushed garlic, thyme and sage.

Place chicken in pot, breast down.

Brown lamb kidneys and mushrooms in the butter in a saucepan, then add sour cream and white wine.

Add mixture to pot, with 1 teaspoon salt, and pepper to taste.

Place covered pot in cold oven.

Set temperature to 480 degrees.

Cook 90 minutes.

Remove pot, pour off liquid into saucepan. If desired, add more sour cream and white wine. Heat and thicken with arrowroot while stirring.

To brown the chicken, return, uncovered, to oven for an additional 5 to 10 minutes of cooking time.

ISRAELI CHICKEN WITH KUMQUATS

(SERVES 4)

1 *frying chicken (3 to 3½ pounds), cut into serving
    pieces*
½ *cup orange juice*
2 *tablespoons lemon juice*
¼ *cup honey*
4 *hot chili peppers, seeded and chopped fine*
10 *to 12 preserved kumquats*

Presoak pot, top and bottom, in water for 15 minutes.

Rub chicken parts with generous amounts of salt, and place
    in pot.

Combine orange juice, lemon juice and honey, and pour over
    the chicken. Add the chilies.

Place covered pot in cold oven.

Set temperature to 480 degrees.

Cook 25 minutes.

Remove from oven, baste chicken with pot liquid and add
    kumquats. Return covered pot to oven and cook additional
    10 minutes.

Remove pot from oven, baste again, and return pot *uncovered*
    to oven for another 10 minutes to brown the chicken.

CHICKEN WITH BROCCOLI

(SERVES 4)

2 tablespoons flour
1½ teaspoons salt
Dash of pepper
½ teaspoon tarragon
1 3-pound frying chicken, cut into serving pieces
2 tablespoons olive oil
Juice of ½ lemon
½ pint sour cream
2 ounces sharp Cheddar cheese
1 pound broccoli, washed, separated and stalks removed

Presoak pot, top and bottom, in water for 15 minutes.

Combine flour, pepper, salt and tarragon in paper bag, add chicken parts and shake. Put aside any remaining flour mixture.

In large frying pan, quickly brown chicken in olive oil until golden.

Place browned chicken in presoaked pot.

Squeeze juice of half a lemon over chicken. Add drippings in frying pan; add sour cream and rest of flour mix. Stir and pour over the chicken. (This should be *thick*.) Grate Cheddar cheese over top.

Place covered pot in cold oven.

Set temperature to 450 degrees.

Cook for 25 minutes.

Remove pot from oven and add the broccoli. Replace covered pot in oven, and cook for additional 10 minutes.

Siphon off excess fat, and serve.

GARVEY'S GARNISHED GALLO,
OR SPANISH SMOTHERED HEN

(SERVES 6)

Al Garvey, one of Marin County's celebrated artists, shares his wife Barbara's passion and skill for whipping up offbeat, exotic dishes that are suggestive of his daring seriographs. Once we made the Garveys devotees of the wet-pot, they adapted it to their own dashing style. This flamboyant contribution is not for the timid, workaday cook! The Garveys claim this will serve six, but we doubt it, especially if there are children around.

12 pieces frying chicken
2 chorizos (hot Spanish) sausages, diced
2 tablespoons flour
2 tablespoons olive oil
1 teaspoon salt
2 red torpedo onions, sliced thin
1 green pepper, sliced thin
1 sweet red pepper, sliced thin
10 black olives, chopped coarse
3 cloves garlic, crushed
1 mango (green as possible), sliced
1 banana, sliced thin
4 pineapple slices, cut into chunks
1 cup of shelled green peas
2 apples, sliced
1 tablespoon salt

1 *teaspoon black pepper*
Arrowroot

Presoak pot, top and bottom, in water for 15 minutes.

Brown the chicken and sausage in a large frying pan with the flour, olive oil and 1 teaspoon of the salt.

Place in pot, and set the frying pan drippings aside.

Add the onions, peppers, olives and garlic to the pot.

Cover the pot and place in a cold oven.

Set temperature at 450 degrees.

Cook 30 minutes.

Remove pot from oven and pour off the liquid into the frying pan with the drippings.

Add to the pot: the mangoes, banana, pineapple, peas, apples, the remaining salt and the pepper.

Return the covered pot to the oven.

Cook an additional 30 minutes.

Meanwhile, heat the liquid and drippings, thicken with arrowroot.

Skim or siphon off excess fat from the sauce before serving.

ROMERTOPF'S BEGGAR'S CHICKEN

(SERVES 3 TO 4)

For teriyaki lovers, here's the finest recipe inspired by the excellent little pamphlet *Cook in Clay* published by the makers of the Romertopf pot. We've served this dish, with variations, to as many as a dozen guests with never anything less than ecstatic results. The chicken comes out tender and full of flavor, especially after being marinated in this incredible sauce. You can add all sorts of Chinese or Japanese seasonings, but be sure they stay on the bland side. Caution: Don't add any salt—there's enough in any good soy sauce. (We prefer the rich, heavy soy sauce bottled in Hong Kong in a brown stone jug by Ko Sang Yick.)

> *1 frying chicken (4 pounds), cut into sections*
> *Arrowroot*

MARINADE:

> *1 teaspoon sesame oil*
> *1 tablespoon dry sherry*
> *¼ teaspoon Chinese Five Spices (see note below)*
> *¼ teaspoon white pepper*
> *1 clove pressed garlic*
> *¼ cup soy sauce*
> *1 teaspoon grated fresh ginger root*

In a non-metal bowl, combine the ingredients for the marinade, mix well, and marinate the pieces of chicken for at least half a day, turning frequently.

When ready to cook, presoak pot, top and bottom, in water for 15 minutes.

Add the chicken and the marinade to the pot.

Place covered pot in a cold oven.

Set temperature to 450 degrees.

Cook 45 minutes.

Ten minutes before end of cooking time, remove the pot and pour off the liquid into a saucepan.

Return the pot to the oven, uncovered, for the final 10 minutes of cooking.

Meanwhile, bring the liquid in saucepan to a boil and thicken with arrowroot.

Serve with rice, liberally drenched with the sauce.

For an optional Chinese touch, sprinkle the chicken with almonds and sesame seeds.

Note: Chinese Five Spices are a combination, in powder form, usually found in Chinese markets. If not available, use star anise, ground to a powder with a mortar and pestle.

ORANGE CHICKEN

(SERVES 4)

No reason why duck should have a monopoly on orange, as this easy-to-fix variation will prove.

1 3- to 4-pound chicken
Salt
Pepper
1 clove garlic, crushed
2 medium oranges, peeled and sliced (reserve the rinds)
½ cup orange juice
¼ cup soy sauce
1 teaspoon grated fresh ginger root
½ teaspoon allspice, ground
1 tablespoon brown sugar
Arrowroot

Presoak pot, top and bottom, in water for fifteen minutes.
Wash chicken, inside and out, under running cold water.
Rub inside of chicken with salt, pepper and pressed garlic.
Stuff with orange slices, peeled.
Place chicken in pot, breast down.
Grate the orange rind and sprinkle over chicken.
Add orange juice, soy sauce, ginger, allspice and brown sugar.
Place covered pot in cold oven.
Turn temperature to 480 degrees.
Cook 90 minutes.
Ten minutes before done, remove from oven, pour liquid into
    saucepan.

Return the pot, uncovered, to oven for final 10 minutes to brown the chicken.

Meanwhile, bring sauce to a boil and thicken with arrowroot.

You may want to add a bit of brown sugar to the sauce, to taste.

GARDEN FRESH CHICKEN BREAST

(SERVES 4)

6 *to 8 chicken breasts, halved*
2 *tablespoons flour*
2 *teaspoons salt*
½ *teaspoon pepper*
2 *tablespoons butter*
1 *clove garlic, crushed*
½ *pound mushrooms, sliced thin*
1 *cup shelled green peas*
2 *bay leaves, whole*
2 *stalks celery, chopped fine*
½ *cup dry white wine*
2 *tablespoons parsley, fresh chopped*

Soak pot, top and bottom, in water for fifteen minutes.

In paper bag, mix flour, salt and pepper. Shake chicken in mixture.

Brown chicken in butter and garlic, put browned chicken in bottom of pot. Add sliced mushrooms, shelled peas, bay leaves and celery.

Heat chicken drippings in saucepan and add white wine and parsley.

Mix well and pour over chicken.

Place covered pot in cold oven.

Set temperature to 480 degrees.

Cook 45 minutes. (Do not overcook.)

CHICKEN WITH CHEESE, SPICES AND BRANDY
(SERVES 4)

This combination brings out the most delightful succulence in the fowl, and the sauce is marvelous poured over rice. You can experiment with the cheese, as long as you use at least 1 cup, unless you prefer a *very* strong cheese. The cheese you prefer in a sandwich is the cheese to use here.

> 3 *pounds chicken parts*
> 1½ *teaspoons salt*
> *Dash of pepper*
> 1½ *teaspoons dried marjoram*
> 1½ *teaspoons dried basil*
> 6 *small white onions*
> ½ *cup brandy*
> 1 *cup grated cheese, of your choice*
> 6 *large mushrooms, sliced*
> ½ *cup chopped fresh parsley*
> *Arrowroot*

Presoak pot, top and bottom, in water for fifteen minutes.
Place chicken parts in pot.
Add salt, pepper, marjoram, basil, onions, and brandy.
Cover with grated cheese.
Top with sliced mushrooms and chopped parsley.
Place covered pot in cold oven.
Set temperature to 480 degrees.

Cook about 75 minutes, or until done.

Remove pot from oven and pour off liquid in saucepan. Heat liquid and add arrowroot to thicken. Serve over rice.

CHICKEN BRIE

(SERVES 4)

You are free to experiment with other kinds of cheese, but the good French Brie gave us one of the best chicken dinners ever.

1 frying chicken (3 to 4 pounds), cut up
2 tablespoons butter
2 tablespoons olive oil
1 tablespoon sesame seeds
2 tablespoons dried basil
2 teaspoons salt
¼ teaspoon black pepper, ground
8 to 10 medium-size mushrooms, sliced thin
1 medium onion, chopped
½ pound French Brie cheese, cut up
½ cup white wine
2 tablespoons brandy
Arrowroot

Soak pot, top and bottom, in water for fifteen minutes.

Brown the cut-up chicken in frying pan with butter and olive oil.

When golden, add sesame seeds, basil, salt and pepper.

Stir well and transfer to presoaked pot.

In the same frying pan, sauté the mushrooms and onions until golden and add to pot.

Top with French Brie cheese, cut up.

To what is left in frying pan, add white wine and brandy, stir and pour into the pot.

Place covered pot in cold oven.

Set temperature to 480 degrees.

Cook 50 minutes.

Pour sauce from pot into frying pan, bring to boil and thicken with arrowroot. Serve sauce with the chicken, and pour over rice.

SWISS CHICKEN WITH MUSHROOMS

(SERVES 4)

> 1 chicken fryer, cut up
> or an equal amount of chicken (parts)
> ¼ cup flour
> ½ teaspoon oregano
> ½ teaspoon marjoram
> ½ teaspoon garlic salt
> 2 tablespoons olive oil
> Salt, to taste
> Pepper, to taste
> 1 teaspoon paprika
> 4 green onions, diced
> 12 to 18 mushrooms, sliced thin
> ¼ cup dry white wine
> ½ pint sour cream
> ¼ pound Swiss cheese

Presoak pot, top and bottom, in water for fifteen minutes.

Shake chicken in bag containing mixture of flour, oregano, paprika, marjoram and garlic salt. Set aside any remaining seasoned flour.

Brown chicken in frying pan—quickly—in olive oil, adding salt and pepper to taste.

Place browned chicken in pot, and add diced onions and sliced mushrooms.

To chicken drippings in saucepan, add white wine and ¼ pint sour cream; heat and thicken with small amount of sea-

soned flour that's left over. Pour over chicken. Salt and
pepper to taste.

Add grated Swiss cheese to chicken.

Place covered pot in cold oven.

Set temperature to 480 degrees.

Cook 45 minutes.

Remove from oven, pour off sauce into saucepan and thicken
with ¼ pint sour cream and small amount of left-over seasoned flour.

Serve with the chicken or over rice.

STUFFED CORNISH GAME HENS

(SERVES 3 TO 6)

3 *Cornish game hens*
Arrowroot

MARINADE:

¼ *cup red table wine*
¼ *cup red wine vinegar*
2 *tablespoons olive oil*
2 *tablespoons Worchestershire sauce*
2 *bay leaves*
1 *clove garlic, pressed*
1 *teaspoon salt*
¼ *cup Curaçao*

STUFFING:

12 *prunes, cooked and chopped*
⅓ *cup brown rice, cooked in 1 cup water*
1 *teaspoon grated fresh ginger root*
1 *teaspoon cloves*
Salt, to taste
Pepper, to taste
1 *onion, chopped fine*

Combine all the ingredients for the marinade (except the Curaçao) and marinate the Cornish game hens for 24 hours, basting often.

When ready to cook, drain the hens, and reserve the marinade.

Combine all the ingredients for the stuffing and stuff the hens.

Pour the reserved marinade into a saucepan and cook under high heat, stirring constantly until marinade is reduced to half its original quantity.

Presoak pot, top and bottom, in water for 15 minutes.

Place hens in the pot and pour over the reduced marinade.

Place covered pot in a cold oven.

Set temperature to 480 degrees.

Cook 45 minutes.

Five minutes before hens are done, remove pot from oven and pour off the liquid into a saucepan.

Return the pot, uncovered, to the oven for the final 5 minutes of cooking.

Meanwhile, bring the liquid to a boil .and thicken with arrowroot, then add the Curaçao and return to a boil.

Serve the sauce over the hens.

CURRIED CHICKEN WITH GUINNESS

(SERVES 4)

Guinness stout and curried chicken go well together. If you can't get the heavy, dark Guinness with the creamy head, use any good dark beer, stout, or ale.

- 1 *frying chicken (2½ to 3 pounds), cut into bite-size pieces*
- 3 *tablespoons flour*
- 3 *tablespoons good Indian curry powder*
- 2 *teaspoons salt*
- 8 *little white onions, peeled*
- 3 *cups cubed pineapple (fresh or unsweetened canned)*
- 1 *green pepper, sliced*
- ⅓ *cup dried currants*
- ¾ *cup Guinness stout (or dark ale)*

Presoak pot, top and bottom, in water for 15 minutes.

Combine flour, curry powder and salt in paper bag, add chicken pieces and shake well. Add remaining flour mixture to the pot, along with all the remaining ingredients. Place chicken on top of vegetables.

Place covered pot in cold oven.

Set temperature to 480 degrees.

Cook 70 minutes. (Remove from oven halfway through cooking and stir contents.)

Serve over rice.

ROAST DUCK À L'ORANGE

(SERVES 4)

1 *duck (5 to 6 pounds), cleaned and giblets reserved*
2 *tablespoons olive oil*
2 *tablespoons paprika*
1 *teaspoon fresh oregano, minced (or ½ teaspoon dried)*
½ *teaspoon fresh rosemary, minced (or ¼ teaspoon dried)*
2 *teaspoons salt*
Pepper, to taste
4 *to 6 small white onions, peeled*
2 *medium oranges*
¼ *cup white wine*
6 *medium carrots, peeled and sliced lengthwise*
Orange Curaçao
1½ *teaspoons arrowroot*

Soak pot in water, top and bottom, for fifteen minutes.
Drain blood from duck and set it aside.
Wash duck thoroughly inside and out under cold running water. Rub salt and pepper inside the duck cavity.
Paint outside of duck with a mixture of olive oil, paprika, oregano and rosemary.
Brown duck in olive oil on both sides.
Stuff inside of duck with small white onions, peeled, and one of the sliced whole oranges.
Place duck in pot, breast down.
Add to pot: innards of duck, sliced carrots, duck's blood, wine, 1 teaspoon salt. Grate the skin of the remaining

orange and sprinkle over duck. Slice remainder of orange and add to pot.

Place covered pot in cold oven.

Set temperature to 480 degrees.

Cook 90 minutes.

Remove pot from oven and pour off liquid into saucepan. Add orange Curaçao. Bring to boil and thicken with arrowroot.

You may want to brown the duck by uncovering it for the last 5 to 10 minutes of cooking. Be sure not to overcook.

BLINDFOLD RABBIT WITH LIVER SURPRISE
(SERVES 3 TO 4)

Americans tend to be weird in their choice of food taboos, but of all our prejudices none seems more bizarre than the rabbit no-no. Long relished by the French as a delicacy, this glorious meat is almost universally spurned on these shores. Hardly anyone we know has tasted rabbit, and you rarely find it displayed on meat counters.

Our aversion to cooking the bunny appears to stem, not from its image as a gentle helpless Easter pet, but from the Depression, when most of us had to make do with whatever was at hand. Often this was the prolific rabbit, whose presence at table conjured up memories of breadlines and the Dust Bowl.

Nothing you can cook in the wet-clay pot will provide such a thrill of discovery. In both taste and texture, rabbit is a cross between sweetbreads and the tenderest of chicken. The bones are small, and the meat is plump, containing more protein and less fat, moisture and calories than chicken, veal, turkey, beef, lamb or pork! And the rabbit liver is, quite simply, the most delicious to be found. Sautéed in butter and bourbon whiskey and served on a cracker, rabbit liver is an incomparable hors d'oeuvre (see below). We call it "blindfold rabbit" because, liver and all, it's a kick to serve incognito—as long as you're sure of your guests!

1 *rabbit, skinned and cut into serving pieces*
3 *tablespoons flour*

2 *tablespoons butter*
2 *tablespoons olive oil*
Salt and freshly ground pepper to taste
1 *large sprig fresh rosemary (or 2 teaspoons dried rose-
    mary)*
1 *teaspoon fresh oregano (or ½ teaspoon dried)*
2 *tablespoons fresh parsley*
4 *tablespoons bourbon*
¼ *cup beef stock or bouillon*
2 *cups Chinese pea pods (optional)*
Arrowroot

Presoak pot, top and bottom, in water for 15 minutes.

Sauté the rabbit pieces in a saucepan with the flour, butter, olive oil, salt and pepper, until brown.

Place browned rabbit in pot and cover with above ingredients.

Place covered pot in cold oven.

Set temperature at 480 degrees.

Cook for 40 minutes.

Ten minutes before completed time, remove pot from oven, pour off liquid into a saucepan.

Return pot, uncovered, for last minutes of cooking to brown rabbit. Bring liquid in saucepan to a boil and thicken with arrowroot.

RABBIT-LIVER HORS D'OEUVRE

Cut rabbit liver into bite-size pieces, and sauté until lightly brown in:

> 2 *teaspoons butter*
> 1 *teaspoon fresh rosemary, finely chopped*
> *Salt and pepper*

Add 1 tablespoon bourbon whiskey to make light sauce. Serve with sauce over cracker or toast.

MONTEREY JACK RABBIT

(SERVES 4)

*1 rabbit, cut into serving pieces with liver and heart
   reserved*
½ cup sauterne
2½ tablespoons butter
1 teaspoon finely chopped fresh rosemary
Dash of brandy
4 tablespoons dark beer
8 small shallots, chopped fine
8 medium mushrooms, sliced thin
1½ teaspoons salt
⅓ cup grated Monterey Jack cheese

Marinate the rabbit pieces at least 4 hours in the sauterne.

When ready to cook, presoak the pot, top and bottom, in water for 15 minutes.

Mince rabbit liver and heart, and sauté in ½ tablespoon of the butter, rosemary and dash of brandy. Set aside.

In a separate saucepan, sauté the rabbit in the remaining 2 tablespoons of butter until lightly browned, add the dark beer and simmer for 5 minutes.

Pour the rabbit, including the liver and heart, and the sauces into the pot.

Add the chopped shallots, sliced mushrooms, salt and grated cheese.

Place the covered pot in a cold oven.

Set temperature at 480 degrees.

Cook 50 minutes, or until tender.

Beef & Veal

ROAST BEEF

(SERVES 6)

ROAST beef steamed in the pot is a different experience. The meat has a delightful texture you can't find in beef cooked any other way.

But one word of caution: It's going to take *much less* time to cook than you think. Rely strictly on your meat thermometer. The size of both the pot and roast will make a difference. If you like your beef rare, check the thermometer after 40 minutes. You can omit the vegetables if you don't want a complete dinner.

5- to 6-pound rolled roast of beef
1 teaspoon salt
Pepper, to taste
6 small white onions, peeled
6 medium carrots, peeled and sliced lengthwise
6 small new potatoes, unpeeled
6 large mushrooms, sliced
3 tablespoons chopped parsley
2 or 3 whole bay leaves
1 teaspoon arrowroot, approximately

Presoak your *largest* pot, top and bottom, in water fifteen minutes.

Trim fat from beef and rub with salt and pepper.

Place beef in pot and insert meat thermometer.

Add to pot all above ingredients, plus 1 teaspoon salt and dash of pepper.

Place covered pot in cold oven.

Set temperature to 480 degrees.

For rare beef, check meat thermometer after 40 minutes. For medium beef, check after 1 hour.

For well-done beef—if you *really* want it that way—check after 90 minutes.

Remove pot from oven when meat thermometer is *almost* up to temperature. (Don't wait until it's right on the nose or it will be overdone.)

Pour liquid into saucepan, bring to boil and thicken with about ½ teaspoon arrowroot.

PANHANDLE BEEF NECK STEW

(SERVES 4)

3 *pounds beef neck, cut into vertebrae sections*
2 *tablespoons flour*
2 *tablespoons olive oil*
2 *tablespoons melted butter*

COMBINE:

2 *cloves garlic, chopped fine*
2 *teaspoons salt*
Juice of ½ lemon
1 *bay leaf*
½ *teaspoon oregano*
½ *can consommé, undiluted*
¼ *teaspoon black pepper*
6 *carrots, sliced lengthwise*
4 *turnips, peeled and left whole*
1 *can solid pack tomatoes, drained*
1 *teaspoon arrowroot, approximately*
3 *tablespoons brandy*
Dash of grated nutmeg

Presoak the pot, top and bottom, in water for 15 minutes.
Dredge the beef neck in the flour, and then place beef in a
large frying pan and brown in the olive oil on all sides.
Place the browned beef neck in the pot.
In the same frying pan, combine the remaining flour with
the melted butter, garlic, salt, lemon juice, bay leaf,
oregano, consommé and pepper. Simmer until thickened.

Meanwhile, add to the pot the carrots, turnips and drained tomatoes. Pour the thickened sauce into the pot.

Place the covered pot in a cold oven.

Set temperature to 450 degrees.

Cook for 90 minutes.

Remove pot from the oven and pour off the liquid into a frying pan. Bring the liquid to a boil and thicken with the arrowroot, then add the brandy and nutmeg.

Serve the sauce separately.

CORNED BEEF AND CABBAGE

(SERVES 4 TO 6)

It took us six months to try corned beef in the pot, afraid it had to be simmered slowly for four hours like all cookbooks advise. But it turned out sumptuous, as usual, with that unique texture we've come to expect from meat cooked the Etruscan way.

Notes of caution: If you're used to cooking corned beef the old way, you'll have a tendency to overcook it in the pot. Use a meat thermometer, if possible, or allow about 35 minutes per pound at 450 degrees. And be sure to trim off all excess fat. *Don't* add any salt! There's more than enough salt in corned beef as is. In fact, the sauce you'll pour off after cooking will be too salty to pour over the meat, as is usually done. Save it as a base for split-pea or lentil soup.

> 4 *pounds corned beef, trim all fat*
> 1 *tablespoon pickling spice*
> 1 *large onion, sliced*
> ⅔ *cup red wine*

Presoak large size pot, top and bottom, in water for fifteen minutes.

Put sliced onion in bottom of pot.

Add corned beef, pickling spice, and wine.

Place covered pot in a cold oven.

Set temperature at 450 degrees.

Cook about 2 hours and 20 minutes (or 35 minutes per pound) or until done according to a meat thermometer.

VARIATION:

One hour before done, remove from oven and add to pot:

> 1 *medium head cabbage, quartered*
> 6 *carrots, sliced*
> 8 *small new potatoes*

Return covered pot to oven and cook until done.

Note: You can substitute or add turnips, parsnips, onions, or rutabagas to the above.

POORBOY POT ROAST

(SERVES 6)

The clay pot has a way of transforming very cheap cuts of meat into miracles of filet-mignon tenderness, especially after marination. See for yourself what it does to the lowly bottom round.

> 3- to 4-pound pot roast, bottom round
> 1 teaspoon sesame oil
> 1 tablespoon soy sauce
> 1 tablespoon vinegar
> 1 tablespoon Marsala wine (or Madeira)
> ½ teaspoon lemon pepper
> 1 teaspoon coarse salt
> ¼ teaspoon curry powder
> 6 medium carrots, peeled and sliced
> 6 small white onions, peeled
> 1 teaspoon arrowroot, approximately

Combine all ingredients—except the carrots, onions and arrowroot—and marinate the pot roast for 3 or 4 days.

When it is about cooking time, presoak the pot, top and bottom, in water for 15 minutes.

Place the roast in the pot along with the marinade, carrots and onions.

Place the covered pot in a cold oven.

Set temperature to 480 degrees.

Cook 70 minutes (for a medium roast).

Remove pot from oven and pour off liquid into a saucepan.

Add the arrowroot and bring to a boil until thickened. Serve the sauce over brown rice.

JEAN BELL'S BEEF STROGANOFF

(SERVES 4)

2 onions, sliced very thin

3 tablespoons flour

1½ teaspoons salt

½ teaspoons freshly ground pepper

1½ pounds top round steak, cut into bite-sized pieces

3 tablespoons cooking oil

1 pint sour cream

2 tablespoons Worchestershire sauce

Juice of 1 lemon

2 tablespoons chopped fresh basil, or 2 teaspoons dried basil

2 bouillon cubes, dissolved in ¼ cup hot water

Presoak pot, both top and bottom, in water for 15 minutes.

Combine the flour, salt and pepper in a paper bag, then add the steak pieces and shake. Set aside any remaining flour mixture. Brown the meat in the cooking oil, then place in pot. Brown the onions in the remaining meat drippings and add to the pot.

To the meat drippings in the frying pan add half the sour cream, the Worchestershire sauce, lemon juice, basil and the dissolved bouillon cubes. Mix well and simmer for a few minutes, then pour over the meat in the pot.

Place the covered pot in a cold oven.

Set temperature at 480 degrees.

Cook for 1 hour.

Test meat for doneness. Pour off liquid into saucepan.

Add the remaining sour cream and thicken, if necessary, with remaining seasoned flour.

Serve over rice or egg noodles.

GERMAN TONGUE WITH FRENCH SAUCE
(SERVES 4 TO 6)

Few dishes come out better in the soaked pot than tongue, especially when doused with this classic French provincial sauce.

On carving: Always slice the tongue crosswise, not lengthwise.

TONGUE:
- 1 fresh beef tongue
- 1 tablespoon pickling spice
- 1 cup beer
- 1 large onion, chopped
- ½ cup white wine
- 2 chicken bouillon cubes, dissolved in ½ cup water, or ½ cup good chicken stock
- 3 cloves garlic, chopped
- 2 teaspoons salt
- ¼ teaspoon freshly ground pepper

SAUCE:
- ¼ cup lingonberry jelly
- 1 cup Madeira wine
- Juice of 1 orange
- 2 slices orange peel
- Juice of ½ lemon
- 2 slices lemon peel
- 1 teaspoon prepared hot mustard (not mustard powder)
- 1 tablespoon grated fresh ginger root

Dash of cayenne pepper
1 tablespoon brown sugar
1½ teaspoons arrowroot, approximately

Place the tongue in a large kettle, add the pickling spices, beer and enough water to cover. Simmer gently for 2 hours.

When about done, presoak pot, top and bottom, in water for 15 minutes.

Put the chopped onion in bottom of the pot, then add the tongue. Combine the white wine, dissolved bouillon cubes, garlic, salt, pepper and ½ cup of the cooking liquid, and pour over the tongue.

Place the covered pot in a cold oven.

Set temperature to 480 degrees.

Cook for 1 hour.

Meanwhile, combine all the ingredients for the sauce, except the arrowroot, and simmer gently in a saucepan for 1 hour while the tongue is in the oven.

After the tongue has cooked in the oven for 1 hour, remove the pot, pour the sauce over the tongue, and return the pot, covered, to the oven for an additional 10 minutes.

Remove pot from the oven, strain the sauce into a saucepan, bring to a boil and thicken with the arrowroot.

To serve, peel off the tongue skin.

Slice tongue crosswise and arrange on a heated platter. Remove the orange and lemon peel from the onion mixture remaining in the pot.

Serve the onion mixture as a side dish, together with the sauce.

HOT DOGS REUBEN STYLE

(SERVES 2 OR 3)

One advantage of wet-pot cookery is that flavor and nutrients remain in the food and aren't boiled away. This is as true of the common hot dog as anything else. You'll find a new kind of frankfurter delight with this method.

> *4 large or 6 small hot dogs*
> *1 pound sauerkraut*
> *¼ pound Swiss cheese*
> *1 teaspoon caraway seeds*

Presoak pot in water, top and bottom, for fifteen minutes.

Drain sauerkraut thoroughly, mix with caraway seeds and place in bottom of pot. Add hot dogs, and slices of Swiss cheese on top.

Place covered pot in cold oven.

Set temperature to 480 degrees.

Cook 30 minutes, or until cheese melts and turns slightly brown.

CZECHOSLOVAKIAN VEAL

(SERVES 4)

3 to 4 tablespoons flour

1 tablespoon salt

1½ tablespoons caraway seeds

1 teaspoon Hungarian paprika

3 pounds veal, cut into cubes

2 tablespoons butter

2 tablespoons olive oil

2 large onions, chopped fine

1 cup fresh mushrooms, thinly sliced

2 chicken bouillon cubes dissolved in ¼ cup water, or ½
    cup chicken stock

¼ cup white wine

Presoak pot, top and bottom, in water for 15 minutes.

Mix the flour, salt, caraway seeds and paprika in a paper
    bag, add the veal cubes and shake.

Brown the veal cubes in a mixture of the butter and olive oil.

Remove from the pan the veal cubes, re-flour, and set aside,
    together with any remaining flour mixture.

In the same saucepan, sauté the onions until golden brown.

Place the veal and the onions into the pot, add the mush-
    rooms, dissolved bouillon cubes (or chicken stock) and
    white wine.

Place the covered pot in the oven.

Set temperature at 450 degrees.

Cook for 50 minutes, or until the veal is tender. Remove pot from the oven, pour off the liquid into a saucepan, heat, and thicken with the leftover seasoned flour.

Note: This dish is traditionally served with buttered egg noodles.

Lamb

RACK OF LAMB

(SERVES 3 TO 4)

With a bit of experimenting, you can cook the entire dinner in one large pot. Put the rack of lamb on top of the vegetables. This will help you to read the meat thermometer; also, if the lamb gets done before the vegetables, simply take the lamb out of the pot and cook the vegetables a bit longer.

1 rack of lamb (2 pounds), trimmed of excess fat
1 clove garlic, crushed
Salt
Pepper, freshly ground
Nutmeg, freshly grated
6 large carrots, peeled and sliced lengthwise
4 large leeks, washed thoroughly and trimmed
8 small new potatoes, unpeeled
¼ cup white wine
2 tablespoons butter
1 teaspoon arrowroot, approximately

Presoak pot, top and bottom, in water for 15 minutes.
Rub the trimmed lamb with the crushed garlic, salt, pepper and nutmeg.
Place all the vegetables in the bottom of the pot, add the

wine and 1 teaspoon salt. Put the lamb on top of the vegetables, insert a meat thermometer, and dot the lamb with butter.

Place the pot, covered, in a cold oven.

Set the temperature at 480 degrees.

Cook 70 minutes, or until thermometer is *almost* up to temperature.

Remove pot from the oven, pour off liquid into saucepan, bring to boil, add 1 teaspoon or more of arrowroot to thicken. If vegetables require more cooking, remove lamb and return covered pot to oven.

Note: You can substitute other vegetables: small white onions or corn on the cob.

LAMB CALYPSO

(SERVES 4 TO 6)

Here's a musty, pungent recipe from the West Indies for the more adventurous cook.

1 leg of lamb (4 pounds), trimmed of excess fat and
    rubbed with salt and pepper
½ cup very strong coffee
¼ cup Curaçao
½ teaspoon orange bitters (optional)
2 tablespoons dark brown sugar
2 tablespoons dark molasses
¼ teaspoon ground mace
½ teaspoon ground cinnamon
¼ teaspoon ground allspice
½ teaspoon salt
¼ teaspoon pepper, freshly ground
A handful of currants

Presoak the pot, top and bottom, in water for 15 minutes.
Insert a meat thermometer in the lamb, away from the bone, and place it in the pot.
Combine all the other ingredients, except the currants, and pour over the lamb. Then sprinkle with the currants.
Place the covered pot in a cold oven.
Set the temperature at 480 degrees.
Cook for 75 minutes, or until done according to the meat thermometer.
Serve the sauce over brown rice.

LEG OF LAMB WITH BLACK WALNUTS

(SERVES 4 TO 6)

Use a large unglazed clay pot for this hearty dish. It needs only a green salad to make a complete dinner.

1 *leg of lamb (4 pounds), trimmed of fat and rubbed with salt and pepper*
1 *teaspoon nutmeg, freshly grated*
4 *pickled black walnuts*
6 *small white onions, peeled*
6 *medium carrots, peeled and sliced lengthwise*
4 *to 6 whole sweet potatoes, or yams*
3 *whole mandarin oranges, unpeeled*
½ *cup orange liqueur*
1 *teaspoon salt*
1 *teaspoon arrowroot, approximately*

Presoak your largest unglazed clay pot, top and bottom, in water for 15 minutes.

Place the prepared lamb in the pot, sprinkle with the nutmeg, then insert a meat thermometer in the lamb, away from the bone. Add all the remaining ingredients, except the arrowroot.

Place the covered pot in a cold oven.

Set the temperature at 480 degrees.

Cook for 2 hours, and then check the meat thermometer. Remove from the oven when the thermometer is *almost* up to temperature.

When the meat is done, pour off the liquid into a saucepan, bring to a boil and thicken with the arrowroot.

Serve the sauce as a side dish.

GREEK LEG OF LAMB WITH ORZO
(RICE-SHAPED PASTA)

(SERVES 6)

1 *leg of lamb (6 to 7 pounds), trimmed of fat*
2 *medium cloves garlic, slivered*
2 *teaspoons dried oregano*
1 *tablespoon salt*
½ *teaspoon freshly ground pepper*
¼ *cup white wine*
Juice of 1 lemon
6 *small white onions, peeled*
3 *green peppers, sliced*
1 *teaspoon arrowroot, approximately*

Presoak the clay pot, top and bottom, in water for 15 minutes.

Make slits in the leg of lamb with a sharp knife and insert the slivers of garlic.

Mix the oregano, salt and pepper and rub over the lamb.

Insert a meat thermometer, away from the bone, and place the lamb in the pot.

Mix the wine and lemon juice and pour over the lamb.

Add the onions and green peppers.

Place the covered pot in a cold oven.

Set the temperature at 480 degrees.

After 60 minutes, check the meat thermometer and cook according to taste, well-done, medium or rare.

When the meat is done, pour off the liquid into a saucepan, bring to a boil and thicken with the arrowroot.

(If lamb is insufficiently browned, remove the lid from the
  pot for the last ten minutes of cooking.)
Serve with orzo (see below).

ORZO:

> 1 *teaspoon salt*
> *Olive oil*
> 2 *cups orzo (rice-shaped pasta)*
> 1 *large onion, chopped fine*
> 2 *tomatoes, chopped fine*
> *Thickened liquid from the roast (see above)*

Bring 1½ quarts of water to a boil with the salt and a little
  olive oil.
When water boils add the orzo a little at a time to keep the
  water boiling.
Cook the orzo about 10 minutes, or until not quite done.
Drain the orzo.
In a saucepan, brown the onions in 1 tablespoon olive oil
  until golden, then add the chopped tomatoes, 1 teaspoon
  salt and all the thickened liquid from the lamb. Stir and
  bring to a strong simmer. Add the orzo and simmer, covered, for 10 minutes.
Serve with the lamb.

TOM BELTON'S LAMB WITH HONEY AND ALMONDS

(SERVES 4 TO 5)

The best pizza on the West Coast is made by a genial red-bearded Irishman in Tiburon, named Tom Belton. He calls his pizzeria "Biagio's," because "who would buy a pizza from a guy called Belton?" Here's his exotic recipe for Lamb with Honey and Almonds which produces a magnificent sauce; what's left over can be used as a stock. Despite what seems to be an imposing list of ingredients, this unique dish is quite easy to make. *All* components are simply mixed together in a large round bowl, and Belton insists that the mixing be done with your *hands*.

*3 pounds boneless shoulder of lamb, trimmed of fat and
        cut into large chunks*
2 large onions, chopped fine
3 tablespoons honey
1 cup raisins
4 carrots, peeled and cut into 1-inch lengths
¾ cup whole almonds
*⅛ teaspoon saffron powder (or ½ teaspoon saffron
        threads)*
1 teaspoon cinnamon
½ teaspoon ground ginger
3 teaspoons salt
Pinch of cayenne pepper
1 large can garbanzo beans, with their liquid

½ *cup water*

1 *teaspoon arrowroot, approximately*

Presoak top and bottom of pot in water for 15 minutes.

Pour *all* ingredients, except the arrowroot, into large round bowl, and mix thoroughly with your *hands*.

Place mixture in presoaked pot.

Place the covered pot in cold oven.

Turn temperature to 450 degrees.

Cook 90 minutes.

Remove pot from oven, pour off the liquid into a saucepan, bring almost to a boil, and thicken with arrowroot.

Serve with brown rice or bulgur. Pour the sauce over both the rice and the lamb.

MOROCCAN LAMB STEW
(TAGINE BAR-BAR)

(SERVES 4)

Al and Barbara Garvey are adventuresome cooks and travelers. Once we turned them on to the unglazed clay pot, they came up with adaptations of recipes they brought back from Morocco.

¼ cup butter (½ stick)

2 tablespoons vegetable oil

2 teaspoons salt

½ teaspoon freshly ground pepper

½ teaspoon ground turmeric

1 teaspoon ground ginger

¾ teaspoon ground cinnamon

3 pounds boneless shoulder of lamb, trimmed of fat and
    cut into 1½-inch chunks

1 large onion, chopped coarsely

1½ cups water

1 pound pitted prunes, soaked if too dry

4 small zucchini, scrubbed and cut into 1-inch lengths

¼ cup freshly chopped parsley

¼ cup chopped fresh coriander, or 2 teaspoons dried
    coriander

½ teaspoon dried thyme

½ teaspoon dried oregano

¼ cup honey

4 tart apples

½ to 1 cup whole blanched almonds

Presoak a clay pot, top and bottom, in water for 15 minutes.

In a saucepan, heat 2 tablespoons of the butter and the oil; add 1½ teaspoons of the salt, the pepper, turmeric, ginger, and ¾ teaspoon cinnamon.

Brown the lamb and chopped onion in this mixture, then transfer to the pot, along with 1½ cups water.

Place the covered pot in a cold oven.

Set temperature at 480 degrees.

Cook for 35 minutes, remove from the oven and add the pitted prunes and the zucchini. Sprinkle with the parsley, coriander, thyme, oregano, the remaining salt and 3 tablespoons of the honey. Cover the pot and return to the oven.

Cook an additional 15 minutes, then check to see if the lamb is done; if not, cook an additional 10 minutes. (Total cooking time: 50 to 60 minutes.)

Meanwhile, core the apples and cut into squares. Sauté the apples and almonds in the remaining butter, along with the remaining honey and a pinch of cinnamon, until the apples are soft, but still slightly firm.

To serve, top the stew with sautéed apples and almonds.

STUFFED LAMB ROLL

(SERVES 5 TO 6)

Boneless rolled shoulder of lamb is one of the many "best buys" in the lamb department. Practically all meat, it's priced at $1.59 a pound (as of January 1974). The easy-to-make stuffing adds a spicy zest to this unusual dish.

- *1 boneless rolled shoulder of lamb (about 4 pounds) trimmed of all fat*
- *1 medium onion, chopped*
- *2 large cloves garlic, crushed*
- *½ cup ripe olives, chopped*
- *3 tablespoons fresh parsley, chopped*
- *½ teaspoon dried marjoram*
- *½ teaspoon fresh rosemary, chopped (or ¼ teaspoon dried rosemary)*
- *2 teaspoons salt*
- *¼ teaspoon fresh ground pepper*
- *½ cup white wine*
- *1 teaspoon arrowroot, approximately*

Presoak a clay pot, top and bottom, in water for 15 minutes.

In a large mixing bowl make a stuffing by combining the onion, garlic, olives, herbs, 1 teaspoon of the salt and the pepper.

If the lamb comes from the butcher rolled and tied, untie and unroll it, then rub both sides of it with the remaining 1 teaspoon of salt.

Spread the stuffing onto the unrolled lamb, roll up tightly and tie with white string.

Place the lamb roll in the presoaked pot and add ¼ cup of the white wine.

Place the covered pot in a cold oven.

Set temperature at 450 degrees.

Cook for 90 minutes (but use your meat thermometer for an accurate guide).

When the lamb is done, remove the pot from oven and pour off the liquid into a saucepan. Heat, add the remaining ¼ cup of white wine, and thicken with the arrowroot.

"HARD TIMES" LAMB BREAST WITH DILL STUFFING

(SERVES 4)

We didn't believe it either, but the lowly, overlooked breast of lamb cost us 39 *cents a pound*, as of January 1974, and turned out a meal as tasty as it was economical.

If lamb breast isn't on display, ask the butcher to fetch it from his meat locker, then tell him to carve a "pocket" suitable for holding stuffing. Be sure to trim as much fat as possible; this may take some time, but the dish is worth it. As Spencer Tracy said of Katherine Hepburn, "There's not much meat on her, but what's there is *cherce!*"

2 *cups unseasoned croutons*
½ *cup chicken stock (or 2 chicken bouillon cubes dissolved in water)*
2 *tablespoons butter*
1 *large onion, chopped fine*
½ *teaspoon freshly ground pepper*
¼ *cup pine nuts*
1 *scant teaspoon dried dill*
1 *large breast of lamb (2 pounds) cut with pocket and trimmed of fat*
½ *cup red wine*
2 *teaspoons salt*

Presoak a clay pot, top and bottom, in water for 15 minutes. In a mixing bowl, soak the croutons in the chicken stock.

Meanwhile, melt the butter in a frying pan and cook the onion until golden brown.

Add to the mixing bowl all the other ingredients, except the lamb, red wine and ½ teaspoon of the salt.

Mix well, then stuff the lamb pocket with the mixture and sew up the opening with unwaxed dental floss.

Rub the surface of the lamb with the remaining salt, then place in the presoaked pot.

Place the covered pot in a cold oven.

Set temperature at 480 degrees.

Cook for 65 to 75 minutes.

When done, pour off the fat and serve the stuffed lamb from the pot.

GREEK BREAST OF LAMB

(SERVES 4)

2 *stalks celery, diced*

3 *medium mushrooms, sliced*

1 *small onion, diced*

1 *tablespoon butter*

1 *tablespoon olive oil*

2 *large cloves garlic, chopped*

2 *teaspoons salt*

2 *tablespoons mint leaves, finely chopped*

1 *teaspoon dried oregano*

¼ *teaspoon freshly ground pepper*

Juice and pulp of ½ lemon

½ *cup rice, half-cooked*

1 *breast of lamb (about 2 pounds), cut with pocket and trimmed of fat*

½ *teaspoon coarse salt*

1 *cup drained canned tomatoes (preferably Italian plum tomatoes)*

2 *bay leaves*

¼ *cup white wine*

1 *teaspoon arrowroot, approximately*

Presoak a clay pot, top and bottom, in water for 15 minutes.

Sauté the celery, mushrooms, and onion in the butter and olive oil. Add the garlic, salt, mint, oregano, pepper and lemon juice.

Cook the rice for *half* the time required by the directions on the package, then combine, cooking liquid and all, with the celery-mushroom mixture.

Mix well, then stuff this mixture into the pocket of the lamb's breast, and sew up the opening with unwaxed dental floss.

Rub surface of the lamb with the coarse salt.

Place the lamb in the presoaked pot, and add the canned tomatoes, bay leaves and white wine.

Place the covered pot in a cold oven.

Set the temperature at 480 degrees.

Cook for 65 to 75 minutes.

When done, remove the pot from the oven and pour off the sauce into a saucepan. Skim or siphon off all fat from the sauce, heat and thicken with the arrowroot. If necessary, remove the bay leaves before serving.

Pork & Ham

·BOAR

PORK ROAST STUFFED WITH SAUSAGE

(SERVES 6)

Here's a rich, cold-weather feast well worth a bit of extra trouble.

STUFFING:

1 medium onion, minced
2 large green apples, peeled and chopped
½ pound bulk pork sausage
4 stalks celery, chopped
3 tablespoons butter
½ cup raisins
1 cup bread crumbs, moistened with water to soften
1 teaspoon salt
Dash of freshly ground pepper
1 teaspoon dried sage
2 teaspoons dried basil

ROAST:

1 boned pork roast (5 pounds) trimmed of fat
½ cup white wine
2 tablespoons honey
1 tablespoon prepared hot mustard

> 1 *teaspoon dried thyme*
> 2 *teaspoons salt*
> ½ *teaspoon pepper*
> 1 *teaspoon arrowroot, approximately*

Sauté the onion and celery in the butter until slightly transparent.

Meanwhile, in a large mixing bowl, combine the chopped apple, the sausage, raisins, 1 teaspoon salt, dash of pepper, the sage and the basil.

Add the moistened bread crumbs, the onion-celery mixture, and combine well.

Presoak a clay pot, top and bottom, in water for 15 minutes.

Fill the cavity of the pork roast with the stuffing and sew up the ends with unwaxed dental floss.

Rub the outside of the roast with a mixture of 2 teaspoons salt, the thyme and ½ teaspoon pepper, then place the stuffed roast in the pot. Insert a meat thermometer into the thickest part of the roast. Combine the wine, honey and mustard and pour over the roast.

Place the covered pot in a cold oven.

Set the temperature at 480 degrees.

Cook for about 2 hours, or until the thermometer is *almost* up to done.

Remove the pot from the oven and pour off the liquid into a saucepan. Skim or siphon the surface fat from the liquid, heat, and thicken with the arrowroot.

PORK LOIN WITH LITTLE GREEN APPLES

(SERVES 4 TO 5)

Sure as God made little green apples, He meant them to go with pork. This recipe calls for pork loin roast, but goes equally well with a fresh, uncooked ham.

You can substitute other vegetables, but we suggest you include the yams or sweet potatoes. (The green apples are, of course, essential.) Your entire dinner can be cooked in one large clay pot.

This is *not* a dish for weight watchers.

1 loin of pork (3 pounds) trimmed of fat

1 clove garlic, crushed

1½ teaspoons salt

½ teaspoon freshly ground pepper

1 large yellow onion, sliced

6 small new potatoes, unpeeled

4 yellow yams or sweet potatoes, unpeeled

6 medium carrots, peeled and sliced lengthwise

6 little green apples, cored

1 sprig fresh rosemary (or 1 teaspoon dried rosemary)

1 tablespoon grated fresh ginger root

3 bay leaves

Brown sugar (enough to fill the cored green apples)

2 tablespoons brandy or rum, approximately

2 tablespoons butter

1 teaspoon arrowroot, approximately

Presoak a clay pot, top and bottom, in water for 15 minutes.

Rub the trimmed pork loin with the garlic, salt and ground pepper. Put the sliced onion in the bottom of the pot, then add the pork loin and insert a meat thermometer.

Place the potatoes, yams and carrots around the pork, leaving room to add the green apples later.

Add the rosemary, ginger, 1½ teaspoons salt and pepper, and top the pork with the 3 bay leaves.

Place the covered pot in a cold oven.

Set the temperature at 480 degrees.

Cook for 1 hour.

Meanwhile, core the green apples, but do not cut through the bottoms. Fill each core with brown sugar, moisten with rum or brandy and top with a pat of butter.

After the 1 hour of cooking time, remove the pot from the oven and place the apples around the roast.

Cover the pot and return to the oven for another hour of cooking (total cooking time, about 2 hours). Check the meat thermometer and remove pot from the oven when the needle is *almost* up to done.

Pour off the liquid into a saucepan, heat, and thicken with the arrowroot.

MEXICAN CHILE VERDE

(SERVES 4)

12 *fresh jalapeña peppers (if you want it hot), or 2*
  four-ounce cans peeled green chilis (if you want it
  mild)
3 *pounds pork loin or tenderloin, cut into ½-inch cubes*
6 *large garlic cloves, crushed*
1 *cube beef bouillon*
½ *teaspoon cumin*
1 *bottle of beer*
3-inch strip orange peel
1 *teaspoon salt*
Avocado slices and sour cream for garnish

Presoak a clay pot, top and bottom, in water for 15 minutes.
If fresh peppers are used, remove the seeds and chop into
  ¼-inch dice. Crush the bouillon cube with the garlic.
Mix all the ingredients together, except the garnish, and place
  in the pot.
Place the covered pot in a cold oven.
Set the temperature at 450 degrees.
Cook for 90 minutes.
Serve in soup bowls garnished with avocado slices and a
  large dollop of sour cream.

GARLIC PORK AND GREEN PEPPERS

(SERVES 4)

You've really got to love garlic, or forget about this one. Here, garlic is the dominant, rather than a casual, flavor. Its origin is British Guiana, birthplace of Ray Handley, whose wife, Louise, submitted this pungent delight for adaptation to the pot. Serve with a good German or Mexican beer— not *too* cold, ever. And mandarin oranges for dessert for the perfect aftertaste.

Note: If you have a Chinese *wok* this is ideal for browning the meat and vegetables before they go into the pot.

>   2 *pounds boneless pork*
>   2 *tablespoons crushed garlic*
>   2 *teaspoons coarse salt*
>   1 *teaspoon freshly ground pepper*
>   2 *large green peppers*
>   3 *large sweet red peppers*
>   *or 2 four-ounce jars pimentoes*
>   1 *large red onion, cut into ½-inch wedges*
>   4 *tablespoons goose or chicken fat, or lard*
>   ½ *cup white wine*
>   1 *tablespoon chicken bouillon concentrate*
>   *or 2 bouillon cubes*
>   1 *teaspoon salt*
>   1 *teaspoon arrowroot, approximately*

Cut the pork in strips ¼-inch thick.
Mash the garlic, coarse salt, and pepper with a mortar and

pestle (or in round bowl with large spoon) until it forms a smooth paste.

With a fine pastry brush, coat both sides of pork strips *lightly* with the garlic paste. Place the strips in a bowl and toss as you would a salad.

Marinate meat in a tightly-closed bowl or jar at room temperature for 3 to 4 hours, churning the strips occasionally to distribute the marinade.

Presoak a clay pot, top and bottom, in water for 15 minutes.

Remove the seeds and white pulp from center of green peppers, and cut into strips an inch wide. Do the same with sweet red peppers, if used.

Place fat or lard in a large heavy skillet (or better, a Chinese *wok*) and bring to high heat. Brown marinated pork strips in hot fat until lightly browned on both sides (about 2 minutes) and remove strips to a plate.

Add the green and red peppers to the hot fat and stir until well covered with fat, but not browned. Remove to a platter. (If pimentoes are used instead of red peppers, these go directly into the pot without coating with fat.)

Add the green and red peppers to the hot fat and stir until golden and slightly transparent.

Place the meat and vegetables in the presoaked pot and stir well.

Add to the frying pan white wine, chicken bouillon concentrate (or cubes), 1 teaspoon salt; stir well and bring almost to a boil, then pour into pot.

Place the covered pot in a cold oven.

Set the temperature at 480 degrees.

Cook 30 to 35 minutes.

Pour off the sauce into hot frying pan and thicken with arrow-root. Serve with brown rice, a good beer and mandarin oranges for dessert.

COUNTRY-STYLE SPARERIBS IN HONEY SAUCE

(SERVES 2 OR 3)

"Country style" spareribs have much more meat on them than the regular lean spareribs used for barbecuing. Ask your butcher for them by name. When cooked with this honey sauce, the country ribs provide one of the most delectable variants in the entire pork family.

3 to 4 pounds country-style spareribs, trimmed of most of the fat
8 medium carrots, peeled and sliced lengthwise
½ cup honey
1 medium onion, chopped fine
Juice of 1 lemon
1 tablespoon good quality curry powder
2 teaspoons salt
½ teaspoon freshly ground pepper
1 teaspoon soy sauce
1 teaspoon arrowroot, approximately

Presoak a clay pot, top and bottom, in water for 15 minutes.
Place the spareribs in the pot, then scatter the carrots on top. Combine the honey, chopped onion, lemon juice, curry powder, salt, pepper and soy sauce in a bowl, mix thoroughly, and pour over the ribs.
Cover the pot and place it in a cold oven.
Set the oven temperature at 480 degrees.
Cook for 70 minutes.

Remove the pot from the oven and pour off the sauce into a sauce pot. Remove the carrots and keep warm until ready to serve.

To brown the ribs return the pot to the oven *without* the lid and cook for an additional 10 minutes. Meanwhile bring the sauce in pan to a boil, add the arrowroot, and stir until thick.

Serve the ribs and carrots covered with the thickened sauce.

EASTER HAM

(SERVES 4 TO 6)

Many of our recipes call for Coleman's dry mustard. This is not to disparage the many excellent spreading mustards from Sweden, France and Germany. But for recipes that call for a dry mustard, we found Coleman's to be consistently without equal.

> 1 *ham (4 pounds)*
> 2 *dozen whole cloves*
> 1 *tablespoon Coleman's dry mustard*
> 2 *tablespoons brown sugar*
> ½ *cup good English marmalade*
> ¾ *teaspoon salt*
> 1 *tablespoon golden sherry*
> 12 *dried prunes*
> 6 *small new potatoes, unpeeled*
> 6 *carrots, peeled and cut in half lengthwise*
> ½ *cup red wine*

Presoak a large clay pot, top and bottom, in water for 15 minutes.

Stick the cloves into the surface of the ham, then place it in the presoaked pot.

Combine the mustard, brown sugar, marmalade, salt, and sherry and coat the surface of the ham with the mixture.

Place the prunes around the ham, then add the new potatoes, carrots, and red wine. Insert the meat thermometer in the ham (away from the bone) and set the dial indicator just below the mark for "precooked ham."

Cover the pot and place it in a cold oven.

Set the oven temperature at 450 degrees.

Cook for 80 minutes, testing for doneness after 1 hour,
Serve with Mustard-Horseradish Sauce (see below).

Note: The liquid will be too salty to serve as a sauce, but
save it for a base for lentil or split-pea soup.

MUSTARD-HORSERADISH SAUCE:
Some things you don't make in the pot. This is one. If you
want to get away from routine store-bought mustard try
this marvel on baked ham, tongue, and hot dogs. It keeps
for weeks in the refrigerator.

> ¼ *cup dry mustard*
> ½ *cup granulated sugar*
> 2 *eggs, beaten*
> ½ *cup light cream (or half-and-half)*
> ½ *cup white vinegar*
> ½ *bottle horseradish (4-ounce size)*

Combine the mustard, sugar, eggs, cream, and vinegar in
a small saucepan.

Bring to a full boil for 2 to 3 minutes, then mix in the horse-
radish. Remove from the heat and stir. Cool before serving.

BAVARIAN HAM

(SERVES 6)

1 precooked ham (5 to 6 pounds), trimmed of all fat
and studded with 1 dozen whole cloves
8 peppercorns
2 bay leaves
1 twelve-ounce bottle of beer

Presoak a large clay pot, top and bottom, in water for 15
minutes.

Insert the meat thermometer in the ham (away from the
bone), then place it, along with all the other ingredients,
into the presoaked pot.

Cover the pot and place it in a cold oven.

Set the oven temperature at 450 degrees.

Cook for 50 minutes, or until the meat thermometer is *just
below* the done mark for precooked ham.

GERMAN POTATO PANCAKES:

This Old World recipe for *Kartoffelpfannküchen* comes from
Georgia's grandmother, and it is one of the few recipes in
this book that does *not* use the clay pot. It makes the perfect
companion for Bavarian Ham cooked in beer (see above)
or Old Munich Sauerbraten on page 176.

2 medium potatoes, peeled and grated
1 large onion, grated
1 egg
1 tablespoon all-purpose flour

1 *teaspoon salt*
1 *teaspoon caraway seeds*
½ *teaspoon granulated sugar*
2 *tablespoons bacon fat*

Combine all the ingredients *except* the bacon fat in a bowl. Heat the bacon fat in a frying pan until *very* hot. Place dollops of pancake batter in hot pan and flatten each until pan is filled with *very* thin 3-inch pancakes. Cook until the underside is golden brown, then turn to brown other side.

Sprinkle with salt, remove from the pan, and keep warm in the oven on paper towels. Continue until all the batter is used up.

Serve with Bavarian ham, sauerbraten and, of course, apple sauce.

Liver, Kidneys &
Sweetbreads

OLD LONDON LIVER AND KIDNEYS

(SERVES 4)

The trick here is to get a *thick* slab of liver, the thicker the better, and not to overcook. Liver is best when cooked to a deep burgundy red, like a properly done wild duck.

> 1 *pound thick unsliced baby beef liver*
> 4 *lamb kidneys, deveined and quartered*
> 4 *medium to large onions, sliced*
> 1 *teaspoon olive oil*
> 1 *tablespoon butter*
> 12 *slices bacon, chopped coarsely*
> ½ *cup chopped fresh parsley*
> 2 *teaspoons salt*
> ½ *teaspoon freshly ground pepper*
> ¼ *cup white wine*
> 1 *teaspoon arrowroot, approximately*

Presoak a clay pot, top and bottom, in water for 15 minutes. Place the liver and kidneys in the presoaked pot. Brown the sliced onions in the butter and olive oil until golden and add to pot, then fry the chopped bacon until almost done, pour off most of the fat and add the bacon to the pot.

Add the chopped parsley, mix thoroughly, then add the salt, pepper, and white wine.

Cover the pot and place it in a cold oven.

Set the temperature at 450 degrees.

Cook for 45 minutes.

Test the liver for a deep red burgundy color, at that point it will be done. (*Do not overcook.*) Remove the pot from the oven and pour off the liquid into a saucepan.

Heat, thicken with the arrowroot, and pour thickened sauce back into pot. Slice the liver just before serving.

Shopping tip: Get the unjustly neglected *lamb's* liver; when last priced it cost $.79 per pound, as opposed to $2.79 for calves', or baby beef liver! And we challenge anyone to tell the difference.

KIDNEYS, MUSHROOMS, AND BROWN RICE
(SERVES 2 TO 3)

This virile dish is simple to prepare, and the brown rice takes
on a surprisingly meaty flavor when steamed together with
lamb kidneys. Don't be tempted to susbtitute white rice; it
may stick to the pot and get mushy—besides, everybody
knows that brown rice tastes better and is better for you.

The recipe calls for shallots, but you can substitute green
onions. Shallots are not always available, and are expensive.
We grow our own; they're as easy to raise as dandelions, and
have it all over green onions in this and many other dishes.

2¼ cups boiling chicken stock, or 2 chicken bouillon
    cubes dissolved in 2¼ cups boiling water
1 small onion, chopped fine
2 teaspoons salt
1 cup raw brown rice
6 lamb kidneys
1 tablespoon vinegar
10 medium-sized whole mushrooms
Pinch of dried thyme
6 shallots or 2 green onions, chopped fine
2 bay leaves
¼ cup red wine

To the boiling chicken stock, add the chopped onion, 1 teaspoon of the salt, and the brown rice. Simmer for 30
minutes. (The rice will *not* be done; it will cook in the
pot.)

Meanwhile cut the kidneys in half and remove the fat and tubes, then plunge into cold water containing the vinegar and soak for 15 minutes.

Presoak a clay pot, top and bottom, in water for 10 minutes.

Place the rice in the bottom of the presoaked pot, then add the kidneys, mushrooms, thyme, shallots, bay leaves, red wine, and remaining salt.

Cover the pot and set it in a cold oven.

Set the temperature at 450 degrees.

Cook for 45 minutes.

ENGLISH BEEF AND KIDNEY PIE

(SERVES 4)

This old English recipe, adapted to the pot, proved a visual as well as gustatory delight when served at the table right from the pot. The brown pastry crust, when punctured, releases a savory cloud of steam that brings on instant salivation. This is among our most successful, and often repeated, adventures with the versatile pot.

FLOUR MIXTURE:

¼ *cup all-purpose flour*
½ *teaspoon dried thyme*
½ *teaspoon dried sage*
½ *teaspoon dried marjoram*
1 *teaspoon salt*
¼ *teaspoon freshly ground pepper*

1 *pound round steak, cut into 1-inch cubes*
1 *pound beef kidneys, cleaned, deveined, and cut into small pieces*
2 *tablespoons bacon fat*
1 *large onion, chopped fine*
6 *large mushrooms, sliced thin*
1 *ten-and-one-half-ounce can condensed beef bouillon*
5 *leeks, cleaned and cut into 2-inch lengths*
6 *carrots, peeled and sliced thin*
4 *small new potatoes, cut in half, unpeeled*
1 *tablespoon chopped fresh parsley*

⅛ cup good quality sherry
Pastry for a 1-crust pie

Presoak a clay pot, top and bottom, in water for 15 minutes.

Combine the flour, thyme, sage, marjoram, salt, and pepper thoroughly in a paper bag, then add the steak and kidneys and shake. Set aside any leftover flour mixture.

Heat the bacon fat in a frying pan and brown the steak and kidneys. Place in the presoaked pot.

In the same frying pan combine the chopped onion, sliced mushrooms (which have been floured in the remaining flour mixture), and the condensed beef bouillon. Simmer for a few minutes, until thickened, then remove from the heat. Add the leeks, carrots, and new potatoes to the pot, then pour the bouillon mixture over and add the chopped parsley and sherry.

Cover with a flaky crust (your own tried and true recipe) and slash the top to allow steam to escape.

Cover the pot and place it in a cold oven.

Set the oven temperature at 480 degrees.

Cook for 1 hour, removing the lid for the last 5 minutes to brown the crust.

Serve right from the pot.

SWEETBREADS WITH HERBS AND MUSHROOMS

(SERVES 2)

Sweetbreads are often hard to come by, and are costly. Many butchers save all their sweetbreads for their restaurant trade, so you might have to pressure your local meat market to put some away for you. They must be absolutely fresh, and served the day they are bought. Sweetbreads always come in pairs and must be thoroughly washed, blanched, and the membranes and tubes removed. This takes a bit of trouble, but as the French say, *"La grande cuisine* cannot wait for man—man must wait for *la grande cuisine."*

The perfect companion for sweetbreads is fresh garden peas, or their frozen equivalent. We prefer to steam fresh vegetables in those round Japanese basket-style bamboo steamers, and peas come out superbly with this method. Put salt and a *few* leaves of fresh rosemary in the water, and you'll never cook peas any other way again.

> 3 *pairs of sweetbreads*
> ¼ *teaspoon salt*
> *Juice of ½ lemon*   *for blanching*
> 6 *medium-sized mushrooms, sliced*
> 1½ *teaspoons salt*
> 1 *tablespoon butter*
> 2 *teaspoons lemon juice*
> 1 *teaspoon chopped chives*
> ¼ *cup chopped parsley*
> ½ *teaspoon dried tarragon*

½ *cup white wine*
1 *teaspoon arrowroot, approximately*

Soak the sweetbreads for at least 1 hour in several changes of cold water, or in slowly running water.

In an enameled or Pyrex pan (*never* in aluminum!), cover the sweetbreads with 2 inches of cold water. Add ¼ teaspoon of the salt and the lemon juice, and blanch by bringing very slowly to the gentlest of simmers and simmering for 15 minutes.

Remove the blanched sweetbreads and plunge into cold water for at least 5 minutes. Carefully remove all the tubes and membranes without tearing the tissues. The sweetbreads are now ready for cooking.

Presoak a clay pot, top and bottom, in water for 10 minutes.

Place the sliced mushrooms in the pot, then add the sweetbreads and all the other ingredients.

Cover the pot and place it in a cold oven.

Turn temperature to 450 degrees.

Cook for 35 minutes.

When the sweetbreads are done, remove the pot and pour off the sauce into a saucepan. Heat, then thicken with the arrowroot. Serve with the sweetbreads.

Fish & Seafood

SAN FRANCISCO CLAMBAKE WITH INSTANT CLAM BROTH

(SERVES 4)

If we had to pick our favorite shellfish recipe, this would win, hands down. The idea is borrowed from the New England clambake: a large pit is dug at the beach and filled with hot stones, then topped with damp seaweed. Into this steamy pit is dumped layers of lobsters, clams, scampi, oysters, scallops, mussels—all in the shell—and sometimes topped with potatoes and ears of sweet corn in the husk. When all these goodies get steamed together, the result is one of the loftiest feasts since man learned to salt his food. The water-soaked pot, when you think of it, is really a clambake in miniature, and it does fabulous things to seafood. The following recipe is open to countless variations. If one type of seafood isn't in season, substitute another.

The sauce manufactured in the wet-pot is not to be thickened—drink it as a broth, or use it as a clam dip. If there's enough left over, save it as a stock for chowder.

1 dozen large prawns (scampi), in the shell
1 dozen scallops
2 dozen clams, in the shell
Juice of 1 lemon

1 *large onion, sliced thin*
4 *small green tomatoes, ground*
¼ *cup dry white wine*
2 *cloves garlic, crushed*
2 *tablespoons chopped fresh parsley*
¼ *teaspoon finely chopped fresh oregano or a pinch of dried oregano*
Pinch of dried basil
2 *tablespoons olive oil*
1 *green pepper, sliced*

Wash all the shellfish in cold running water.

Presoak a clay pot, top and bottom, in water for 15 minutes.

Line the bottom of the presoaked pot with sliced onion, then add the clams. Top with the shrimp and scallops, then squeeze the lemon juice over. Add all the remaining ingredients.

Cover the pot and place it in a cold oven.

Set the oven temperature to 450 degrees.

Cook for 40 minutes.

When done, pour the liquid into small soup cups—do not thicken—and serve as a soup or clam dip.

Serve with saffron rice cooked with pine nuts and pimentoes.

Note: Enhance this dish with a good-quality German white wine (not the too-sweet Liebfraumilch or Moselblumchen) or Charles Krug's excellent California Chenin Blanc, Traminer, or Gewürztraminer.

SALMON WITH SOUR CREAM

(SERVES 6)

1 section salmon (4 to 6 pounds)
¼ cup chopped parsley
1 tablespoon chopped fresh tarragon or 1 teaspoon dried tarragon
1 medium tomato, sliced
1 onion, sliced
1 teaspoon salad oil or good-quality French dressing
½ lemon, sliced
¼ cup white wine
Salt and freshly ground pepper to taste
½ cup sour cream
1 tablespoon capers
1 teaspoon arrowroot

Presoak a clay pot, top and bottom, in water for 15 minutes.

Place the salmon in the presoaked pot and add the parsley, tarragon, tomato, onion, oil, lemon, white wine, salt, and pepper.

Cover the pot and place it in cold oven.

Set the oven temperature at 480 degrees.

Cook 10 minutes for each inch of thickness of salmon, plus 15 minutes for the pot. Test the salmon for doneness by lifting the section away from bones—it should separate freely. Don't overcook! When done, pour off the liquid into a saucepan, heat to boiling and add the sour cream, capers, and arrowroot. Stir until thickened and serve over the salmon.

POACHED SALMON PROVENCALE

(SERVES 4)

1 *salmon (4 to 5 pounds), in sections*
Salt and freshly ground pepper
1 *lemon, unpeeled and sliced*
1 *medium onion, sliced*
2 *stalks celery, sliced*
2 *bay leaves*
1 *tablespoon chopped fresh tarragon or 1½ teaspoons dried tarragon*
½ *cup dry white wine*
3 *tablespoons olive oil*
3 *tablespoons chopped fresh parsley*
¼ *cup mayonnaise*
1 *egg yolk*
Dash of prepared mustard
⅛ *teaspoon dried dill*
½ *teaspoon capers*
Juice of ¼ lemon
1 *teaspoon arrowroot, approximately*

Presoak a clay pot, top and bottom, in water for 15 minutes. Enlarge the opening in the salmon cavity and rub the salmon, inside and out, with salt and pepper. Insert half the lemon slices, half the celery, and half the onion in the cavity, place in the clay pot and add the remaining lemon slices, celery, and onion on top of the salmon. Add the bay leaves, tarragon, white wine, olive oil, and parsley.
Cover the pot and place in a cold oven.

Set the oven temperature at 450 degrees.

Cook for 45 minutes.

Meanwhile, combine the mayonnaise, egg yolk, mustard, dill, capers, and lemon juice. Set aside.

After 45 minutes test the fish for doneness; it should lift easily away from the bones (*don't overcook*). When it is done, remove the pot from the oven and pour off the liquid into a saucepan, heat, and thicken with the arrowroot. Add the reserved mayonnaise mixture, mix well, and serve with the salmon.

SALMON POACHED IN BEER

(SERVES 4)

Cooking in wine is taken for granted, but the overlooked bottle of beer can coax surprising subtleties from all sorts of dishes, especially salmon. Jack and Barbara Thomas of Seattle provided this recipe, which we adapted to the clay pot.

> 4 *salmon steaks*
> 2 *tablespoons melted butter*
> ¼ *cup chopped parsley*
> ½ *teaspoon salt*
> 1 *clove garlic, crushed*
> 1 *teaspoon lemon juice*
> ½ *cup beer*
> 1 *teaspoon arrowroot, approximately*

Presoak a clay pot, top and bottom, in water for 15 minutes.

Place the salmon steaks in the presoaked pot. Combine the melted butter, parsley, salt, garlic, lemon juice, and beer and pour over the fish.

Cover the pot and place it in a cold oven.

Set the oven temperature at 450 degrees.

Cook for 30 minutes.

Remove the pot from the oven and pour off the liquid into a saucepan. Return the pot to oven, without the lid, for an additional 5 minutes, to brown the salmon. Meanwhile, heat the liquid and thicken it slightly with the arrowroot.

SALMON STEAKS

(SERVES 4)

All fish take to the pot: salmon seems to take a little better. We like to marinate the salmon for several minutes in lemon juice before cooking to keep the fish from crumbling. Be careful not to overcook: the meat will hold together and the flavor will be enhanced with minimal cooking time.

2 tablespoons olive oil
Juice of 1 lemon
3 teaspoons crushed rosemary, preferably garden fresh
4 salmon steaks (each 1 inch thick)
6 medium mushrooms, sliced thin
1 onion, sliced thin
½ cup white wine
Plenty of chopped fresh parsley (hard to overdo this!)
1 teaspoon salt
Pinch of freshly ground pepper
1 teaspoon arrowroot, approximately
½ cup sour cream

Presoak a clay pot, top and bottom, in water for 15 minutes.
Combine the olive oil, lemon juice, and crushed rosemary. Paint the salmon with the mixture, then place in the presoaked pot. Add the mushrooms, onion, white wine, parsley, salt, and pepper.
Cover the pot and place it in a cold oven.
Set the oven temperature at 450 degrees.
Cook for 40 minutes.

Five minutes before cooking time is up, remove the pot from the oven and pour off the sauce into a saucepan. Return the covered pot to the oven for the last 5 minutes.

Meanwhile, heat the sauce to boiling, reduce heat, add arrowroot and sour cream, and stir until thick.

SAUSALITO RED SNAPPER

(SERVES 4)

2 *slices bacon, minced*
1 *small clove garlic, crushed*
2 *tablespoons chopped fresh parsley*
½ *small onion, minced*
2 *tablespoons olive oil*
4 *thick slices red snapper*
Cayenne pepper
¼ *cup dry white wine*
6 *capers*
1 *teaspoon minced fresh tarragon or ½ teaspoon dried tarragon*
1 *teaspoon Worcestershire sauce*
Dash of Tabasco sauce
Juice of ½ lemon
1 *teaspoon arrowroot, approximately*

Presoak a clay pot, top and bottom, in water for 15 minutes.
Sauté the bacon, garlic, parsley, and onion in the olive oil until golden brown, then paint the mixture on both sides of each snapper slice, adding a dash of cayenne to each side.
Combine the white wine, capers, tarragon, Worcestershire sauce, Tabasco, and lemon juice in a saucepan. Bring to a boil while crushing the tarragon and capers. Place the fish in the presoaked pot and cover with the sauce.
Cover the pot and place it in a cold oven.

Set the oven temperature at 450 degrees.

Cook for 30 minutes.

Remove the pot from the oven and pour off the liquid into a saucepan. Heat the liquid and add the arrowroot to thicken, then pour the sauce back into the pot. Return the pot to the oven, without the lid, for 5 minutes to brown the fish.

HALIBUT WITH MUSHROOM AND ANCHOVY SAUCE

(SERVES 6)

1 *section halibut (4 to 6 pounds)*
¼ *cup chopped fresh parsley*
2 *bay leaves*
1 *small onion, sliced*
½ *lemon, sliced*
2 *tablespoons olive oil*
¼ *cup white wine*
Salt and freshly ground pepper to taste
6 *mushrooms, sliced thin*
1 *onion, chopped fine*
2 *tablespoons anchovy paste*
2 *tablespoons butter*
1 *teaspoon arrowroot, approximately*

Presoak a clay pot, top and bottom, in water for 15 minutes.

Put the halibut in the presoaked pot; add the parsley, bay leaves, onion slices, lemon, olive oil, white wine, salt, and pepper.

Cover the pot and place it in a cold oven.

Set the oven temperature at 480 degrees.

Cook for 10 minutes for each inch of halibut thickness, plus 15 minutes for the pot. (Don't overcook!) When done, remove the pot from the oven and pour off the liquid into a saucepan. Heat to boiling.

Meanwhile, in a separate pan, sauté the sliced mushrooms

and chopped onion in the butter along with the anchovy paste, then add to the halibut sauce. Add the arrowroot and stir until thickened. Pour over the fish and serve.

ROCK COD IN A HURRY

(SERVES 3 TO 4)

Here's your basic steamed fish recipe for cooks with no time to spare. Other kinds of fish can be substituted, but we urge you to try it with rock cod. This one is simple, quick, and hard to improve.

> 3 *pounds rock cod*
> 1 *lemon*
> 2 *tablespoons melted butter*
> *White wine*
> 1 *onion, sliced thin*
> 6 *medium mushrooms, sliced thin*
> *Salt and freshly ground pepper to taste*
> *Capers*
> 1 *teaspoon arrowroot, approximately*

Presoak a clay pot, top and bottom, in water for 15 minutes.

Wash the fish in cold running water, then squeeze the juice of lemon over the fish and let stand while the pot is soaking. Set the juiced lemon aside.

When ready to cook, brush the fish with the melted butter. Slice the reserved juiced lemon and place it both inside and outside of the fish. Place the fish in the pot; add ¼ cup white wine, onion, mushrooms, salt, and pepper.

Cover the pot and put it in a cold oven.

Set the oven temperature at 450 degrees.

Cook for 45 minutes.

Five minutes before the cooking time is up, remove the pot from the oven and pour off the liquid into a saucepan, return the uncovered pot to the oven for the last 5 minutes of cooking time to brown the fish.

Meanwhile, add a dash of white wine and the arrowroot to the liquid and stir until thickened. Add capers to taste.

OYSTERS FLORENTINE

(SERVES 2 TO 3)

2 *bunches fresh spinach, cleaned and chopped fine*
18 *or more oysters, cleaned and shucked*
¼ *pound sharp Cheddar cheese, sliced*
1 *teaspoon capers*
2 *tablespoons melted butter*
Juice of ½ lemon
1 *teaspoon salt*
Dash of cayenne
1 *teaspoon arrowroot, approximately*

Presoak a clay pot, top and bottom, in water for 15 minutes.

Place the freshly chopped spinach in the bottom of the pre-soaked pot.

Top with the oysters, then cover with the sliced Cheddar cheese and sprinkle with the capers.

Combine the melted butter, lemon juice, salt and cayenne and pour over the oysters.

Cover the pot and place it in a cold oven.

Set the oven temperature at 450 degrees.

Cook for 30 minutes, then remove the pot from the oven and pour off the liquid into a saucepan. Return the pot to the oven, uncovered, for 5 minutes to allow the cheese to brown.

Meanwhile, bring the liquid in the saucepan to a boil, add the arrowroot, and stir until thickened.

SLIGHTLY ITALIAN OYSTERS

(SERVES 4)

Here's a totally improvised dish that delighted post-Yuletide guests surfeited with Christmas fowl. Be sure to place the oysters in the center, and don't overcook. Instead of olive oil, we used goose fat left over from the Christmas goose.

> 2 pints shucked oysters, liquid reserved
> 1 medium-sized eggplant, sliced
> 1 tablespoon olive oil or goose fat
> 2 medium-sized onions, sliced thin
> 1 tomato, sliced
> ¾ pound Monterey Jack cheese, sliced
> ½ cup bread crumbs or crushed melba toast
> 2 teaspoons dried oregano
> Dash of cayenne
> ¼ teaspoon freshly ground black pepper
> 2 teaspoons salt
> 1 teaspoon Maggi seasoning

Presoak a clay pot, top and bottom, in water for 15 minutes. Fry the sliced eggplant in 2 teaspoons olive oil (or goose fat) and set aside, fry the thinly sliced onions in the remaining olive oil and set aside. Place alternate layers of half the eggplant, the sliced tomato, onions, and half the cheese in the presoaked pot. Place the oysters in the center and top with the remaining eggplant and cheese, bread crumbs, and seasonings. Combine the oyster liquid with the Maggi seasoning and pour over.

Cover the pot and place it in a cold oven.

Set the oven temperature at 450 degrees.

Cook for 30 minutes.

Remove the top for the last 5 minutes of cooking to brown.

OYSTERS ROCKEFELLER—WITH VARIATIONS

(SERVES 4)

For the oyster lover, here is a fabulous variation. If you don't relish oysters (it always surprises us how many people don't), try this anyway.

The trick is not to skimp on the oysters—they disappear like so many salted peanuts. Bottled oysters, if *very* fresh, will do, but of course it's better to get them alive in the shell and shuck them yourself. The notion of eating oysters live is repellent to some, but the French won't eat them any other way; when the Gauls open the shell, they prod the bivalve in the erogenous zone with a small fork—if the beast doesn't jiggle, it goes down the sink. The live ones slither wiggling down the gullet. Of course, no oyster will survive a baking in the wet-pot, but it's good to know he was alive just before he was popped in the oven.

2 large bunches fresh spinach, cleaned and shredded
18 to 24 (or more) large oysters, shucked, liquid reserved
¼ stick butter
1 teaspoon salt
½ teaspoon freshly ground pepper
½ teaspoon freshly grated nutmeg
2 cloves garlic, crushed
¼ cup white wine
½ cup freshly grated Parmesan cheese
2 teaspoons arrowroot, approximately
½ cup light cream or half-and-half

1 *tablespoon anchovy paste*
3 *tablespoons Pernod or 2 tablespoons anisette*
4 *thin slices French bread, toasted*

Presoak a clay pot, top and bottom, in water for 15 minutes.

Place the shredded spinach on the bottom of the presoaked pot.

Combine the butter, salt, pepper, nutmeg, garlic, and wine in a saucepan, heat until well mixed, and pour over the spinach.

Add the oysters and sprinkle with Parmesan cheese.

Cover the pot and place it in a cold oven.

Set the oven temperature at 450 degrees.

Cook for 35 minutes, then remove from the oven and pour off the sauce into a saucepan. Return the pot, uncovered, to the oven for another 5 minutes to allow the cheese to brown.

Meanwhile bring the liquid in the saucepan to a boil; add the butter and the arrowroot mixed with the light cream, the reserve oyster liquid, anchovy paste, and Pernod. Stir until thick.

Place the spinach and oysters on the toasted French bread and cover with the sauce.

Note: This is excellent when served with green salad and small buttered, parsleyed new potatoes.

SEA BASS

ITALIAN STYLE

(SERVES 4)

1 *medium onion, sliced thin*
1 *green pepper, deveined, seeded, and sliced*
4 *medium mushrooms, sliced thin*
4 *slices sea bass (2½ pounds)*

COMBINE:

1 *teaspoon salt*
1 *clove garlic, minced*
½ *teaspoon dried oregano*
½ *teaspoon dried marjoram*
½ *cup tomato sauce*
½ *cup fish stock*
1½ *teaspoons arrowroot, approximately*

Presoak a clay pot, top and bottom, in water for 15 minutes.

Place the onion, green pepper, and mushrooms in the bottom of the presoaked pot, lay the slices of bass on top. Combine the salt, garlic, herbs, tomato sauce, and fish stock and pour over the fish.

Cover the pot and place it in a cold oven.

Set the oven temperature at 450 degrees.

Cook for 45 minutes.

When done, remove the pot from the oven and pour off the sauce into a heated saucepan. Heat and thicken with the arrowroot.

HERB-STUFFED SQUID

(SERVES 4)

1 *dozen squid*
2 *tablespoons olive oil*
2 *tablespoons butter*
1 *onion, chopped fine*
½ *teaspoon salt*
Pinch of freshly ground pepper
¼ *cup chopped fresh parsley*
3 *tablespoons chopped fresh basil*
or 2 teaspoons dried basil
2 *cloves garlic, crushed*
½ *cup bread crumbs*
¼ *cup water, approximately*
Juice of ½ lemon
1 *tablespoon sherry*
2 *tablespoons white wine*

Presoak a clay pot, top and bottom, in water for 10 minutes. Clean the squid, removing the purple membrane and translucent cartilage and leaving the body and tentacles whole, discarding the head. In a frying pan, heat the olive oil and butter and sauté the chopped onion until golden. Add the salt, pepper, parsley, basil, garlic, and bread crumbs, then add enough water (about ¼ cup) to soften the bread crumbs and make a stuffing that holds together. *Lightly* stuff the squid (the casing will break if packed too full) with the mixture and close with toothpicks. Place the stuffed squid and whole tentacles in the presoaked pot, then squeeze the lemon juice over the squid and add the sherry and white wine.

Cover the pot and place it in a cold oven.

Set the oven temperature at 480 degrees.

Cook for 30 minutes, removing the lid for the last 5 minutes of cooking to brown.

Vegetables & Vegetable Casseroles

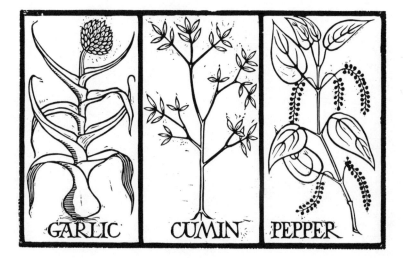

GARLIC   CUMIN   PEPPER

STUFFED ZUCCHINI

(SERVES 4 TO 6)

Get the largest zucchini you can find—if you grow your own as we do, then they can grow to watermelon size. Zucchini are absurdly easy to grow from seeds, and no store-bought vegetable can ever compare with that picked "live" from your own garden, either in taste or aroma. Also, don't neglect the lovely orange flowers that outnumber the zucchini; they are marvelous when French-fried, and many gourmets prefer them to the vegetable itself.

> *1 large zucchini*

FOR STUFFING COMBINE:

> *1 large onion, grated*
> *⅓ cup cooked rice*
> *½ cup canned tomato sauce*
> *¼ teaspoon salt*
> *½ teaspoon dried oregano*
> *1 small clove garlic, chopped fine*
> *¼ cup freshly grated Parmesan cheese*
> *¼ cup chicken stock*

Presoak a clay pot, top and bottom, in water for 10 minutes.

Cut a narrow slice out of the zucchini lengthwise and hollow out the inside. Chop the scooped out flesh and set aside.

In a large mixing bowl, combine the onion, rice, tomato sauce, salt, oregano, and garlic and add the reserved chopped zucchini flesh.

Stuff the zucchini shell with the mixture and place in the presoaked pot. Add chicken stock. Sprinkle with the grated Parmesan cheese.

Cover the pot and place it in a cold oven.

Set the oven temperature at 450 degrees.

Cook for 45 minutes.

BAKED ZUCCHINI

(SERVES 3 OR 4 AS A SIDE DISH)

2 *cups whipped cottage cheese*
½ *teaspoon dried oregano*
½ *teaspoon dried basil*
   or 2 tablespoons fresh chopped basil
¼ *teaspoon salt*
Pinch freshly ground pepper
5 *to 6 small zucchini, scrubbed and cut into ½-inch rounds*
½ *cup freshly grated Parmesan cheese*

Presoak a clay pot, top and bottom, in water for 15 minutes.

Combine the cottage cheese, herbs, salt, and pepper. Put a third of the zucchini slices in the bottom of the presoaked pot and top with half the cottage cheese mixture. Add another third of the zucchini slices, top with the remaining cottage cheese mixture, and put the remaining zucchini on. Sprinkle with the Parmesan cheese.

Cover the pot and place it in a cold oven.

Set the oven temperature at 450 degrees.

Cook for 50 to 55 minutes.

GERMAN SWEET-AND-SOUR RED CABBAGE

(SERVES 6 TO 8)

With potato pancakes and apple sauce, here's the fit companion for the Old Munich sauerbraten on page 176.

4 slices bacon, chopped
1 medium-sized head red cabbage, chopped fine
2 medium onions, chopped fine
2 medium green apples, cored and chopped fine
1 cup water
¼ cup cider vinegar (must be cider), more if necessary
¼ cup brown sugar, more if necessary
1 teaspoon salt
¼ teaspoon freshly ground pepper

Presoak a clay pot, top and bottom, in water for 15 minutes.

In a large frying pan, fry the chopped bacon until crisp, then remove from the pan, drain on a paper towel, and set aside.

Sauté the cabbage in the bacon fat for 5 to 6 minutes, or until slightly limp, then place in the presoaked pot. Add the chopped onions and apples.

Combine the water, cider vinegar, brown sugar, salt, and pepper, and mix in with the contents of the pot.

Cover the pot and place it in a cold oven.

Set the oven temperature at 480 degrees.

Cook for 30 minutes.

When done, mix in the fried bacon, taste for the correct "sweet and sour" quality. If necessary add more brown sugar if too sour, or more vinegar if too sweet.

STUFFED EGGPLANT

À LA PEGGY HARVEY
(A VEGETABLE DELIGHT SERVING 2 TO 4)

Peggy Harvey, former Powers model, wrote one of our favorite and most readable cookbooks, *Season to Taste.*°
Here's her recipe for eggplant casserole adapted to the clay pot. Its natural serving companion is leg of lamb.

> 1 *large eggplant*
> 10 *soda crackers*
> 2 *tablespoons butter*
> ¼ *pint sour cream*

Simmer the eggplant in a large pot of water until tender, about 1 hour.

When about ready to cook, presoak a clay pot, top and bottom, in water for 15 minutes.

Cut the eggplant in half and carefully remove the pulp, setting the skin aside.

Mash the pulp with the soda crackers, butter and sour cream, then refill the skin and place in the clay pot.

Place the covered pot in a cold oven.

Set the temperature at 480 degrees.

Cook for 35 minutes.

° Alfred A. Knopf, Inc., 1957.

EGGPLANT "IMAM BAALDI"

Imam Baaldi isn't a man's name, but Turkish for "The priest has fainted!" According to the ancient legend, when this dish was first served to a certain priest, he passed out from sheer joy.

The dish should be served *very* cold; so refrigerate for one day before serving.

> 1 *large eggplant*
> 2 *tomatoes*
> 1 *onion*
> 7 *tablespoons olive oil*
> ¼ *cup currants*
> *Salt and freshly ground pepper*
> 2 *teaspoons chopped fresh thyme*
>   *or ½ teaspoon dried thyme*
> 2 *fresh bay leaves, crushed*
>   *or ½ teaspoon dried, powdered bay leaf*

Presoak a clay pot, top and bottom, in water for 15 minutes. Cut the eggplant in half. Carefully scoop out most of the pulp without damaging the skin, then set the skins aside. Chop the eggplant pulp, tomatoes, and onions and fry the mixture in 3 tablespoons olive oil until tender and the onion is transparent. Add the currants, then fill the reserved eggplant skins with the mixture. Sprinkle with salt and pepper to taste. Place in the presoaked pot, add ½ cup of water to the bottom. Blend the remaining olive oil, the thyme, the bay leaves, and sprinkle over the top.

Cover the pot and place it in a cold oven.

Set the oven temperature at 450 degrees.

Cook for 75 minutes.

The eggplant should be quite soft. Serve very cold.

TOMATOES STUFFED WITH MUSHROOMS

(SERVES 4)

3 to 4 red tomatoes, very firm
2 tablespoons butter
½ pound mushrooms, sliced thin
Juice of ½ lemon
Salt and freshly ground pepper
1 tablespoon Worcestershire sauce
4 shallots, chopped
1 egg yolk
4 soda crackers, crushed
Freshly grated Parmesan cheese

Presoak a clay pot, top and bottom, in water for 15 minutes.
Remove the top, seeds and pulp from tomatoes. Dry the
tomato shells, then set both shells and pulp aside.

Melt the butter in a frying pan and sauté the sliced mushrooms, along with the lemon juice, and salt and pepper
to taste, over high heat, stirring constantly until slightly
dry. Remove from the heat when you begin to note the
unique odor. Add the tomato pulp, Worcestershire sauce,
and the shallots, which have been mixed with the egg
yolks, and cook for an additional 5 minutes. Mix with the
crushed crackers, then fill the reserved tomato shells.
Sprinkle with the Parmesan cheese and place in the presoaked pot.

Cover the pot and place it in a cold oven.

Set the oven temperature at 480 degrees.

Cook for 30 minutes.

During the last 5 minutes of cooking, remove the lid and pour off the juice. Save the juice for soup stock.

MIDDLE EASTERN EGGPLANT CASSEROLE
(SERVES 4 AS A MAIN COURSE)

2 *medium-sized eggplants*
2 *medium onions, chopped fine*
2 *tablespoons olive oil*
2 *ripe tomatoes, coarsely chopped*
2 *tablespoons pesto (see below)*
1 *teaspoon salt*
½ *pound sharp Cheddar cheese, sliced thin*
8 *soda crackers*
3 *tablespoons freshly grated Parmesan cheese*

Presoak a clay pot, top and bottom, in water for 15 minutes.
Slice the eggplant, unskinned, very thin and set aside, brown
the finely chopped onion in the olive oil until transparent.
Put the tomatoes, pesto, and salt into a blender container
and blend. To this mixture add the onions and remaining
olive oil.
In the presoaked pot, place alternate layers of sliced eggplant, sliced cheese, tomato-onion mixture, and crumbled
soda crackers. When all the ingredients are layered, sprinkle the top with the Parmesan cheese.
Cover the pot and place in a cold oven.
Set the temperature at 480 degrees.
Cook for 45 minutes.

PESTO:

We make our own pesto from garden basil. You can, of
course, buy basil in most markets—in season. But the home-

grown variety adds that pungent, earthy zing that leaps at the nostrils.

You'll soon get addicted to this heavenly green Italian sauce that does so much to enhance sliced tomatoes, pasta, and even potato salad. Pesto will keep for several weeks in the refrigerator if you float a layer of olive oil on top.

> ¾ *cup fresh basil leaves, stems removed*
> ½ *cup chopped parsley*
> ¾ *teaspoon salt, more if necessary*
> 2 *large cloves garlic*
> ⅓ *cup pine nuts*
> ¾ *cup olive oil*
> ⅓ *cup freshly grated Parmesan cheese*

Place basil and parsley, salt, garlic and pine nuts in a blender container, add the olive oil and blend.

Taste and adjust salt, then add the Parmesan cheese and blend again. The sauce should have the consistency of heavy cream.

KENTUCKY GREEN BEANS WITH ALMONDS

(SERVES 4)

Here's an exemplary vegetable delight to serve with almost any meat dish, especially those that take the same time and temperature (450 degrees for 1 hour). Put the bean dish in your small clay pot, the meat dish in a large one and cook them at the same time.

1 *pound Kentucky Wonder green beans, French sliced*
¼ *cup blanched (white) slivered almonds*
1 *ten-and-one-half-ounce can cream of mushroom soup*
½ *cup white wine*

Presoak a small clay pot, top and bottom, in water for 15 minutes.
Place beans in the presoaked pot, and top with the almonds.
Combine the soup with white wine and add to the pot.
Cover the pot and place it in a cold oven.
Set the oven temperature at 450 degrees.
Cook for 1 hour.

EGGPLANT-CHEESE WITH SPANISH SAUSAGE

(SERVES 3 OR 4)

1 *large eggplant, sliced ¼-inch thick*
3 *tablespoons olive oil*
4 *hot, spicy Spanish or Italian sausages, sliced ½-inch thick*
1 *cup crushed seasoned croutons*
1 *teaspoon dried marjoram*
1 *teaspoon dried oregano*
2 *large cloves garlic, crushed, or ½ teaspoon garlic powder*
1 *teaspoon salt*
2 *large tomatoes, sliced*
⅓ *pound sharp Cheddar cheese, sliced*
8 *green onions, chopped*
⅓ *cup freshly grated Parmesan cheese*

Presoak a clay pot, top and bottom, in water for 15 minutes.
Fry the sliced eggplant in the olive oil until slightly transparent, then remove and set aside. Brown the sliced sausages, and set aside. Mix the crushed croutons with the marjoram, oregano, garlic, and salt.
In the presoaked pot, place alternate layers of sausage, tomatoes, eggplant, sliced Cheddar cheese, green onions, and crouton-herb mixture. When all the ingredients have been layered, sprinkle the Parmesan cheese over the top.
Cover the pot and place it in a cold oven.
Set the oven temperature at 450 degrees.

Cook for 50 minutes.

Test for doneness, then return the pot, uncovered, to the oven and brown for about 5 minutes.

Serve right from the pot.

EGGPLANT WITH HAM AND CHEESE

(SERVES 4)

1 *large eggplant, sliced thin*
¼ *pound French Brie or other soft, mild cheese, sliced*
4 *large stalks broccoli, chopped coarsely*
¼ *pound precooked ham, chopped coarsely*
½ *cup crushed soda crackers*
¼ *cup freshly grated Parmesan cheese*

FOR SAUCE COMBINE:

1 *eight-ounce can tomato sauce*
2 *large cloves garlic, crushed*
1 *tablespoon olive oil or butter*
½ *teaspoon salt*
¾ *teaspoon dried oregano*
¾ *teaspoon dried basil*

Presoak a clay pot, top and bottom, in water for 15 minutes.

Brown the thinly sliced eggplant in a frying pan with a little oil or butter (if using a Teflon pan, no oil is needed), then set aside.

In the presoaked pot, place alternate layers of eggplant, ham, cheese, broccoli, cracker crumbs, and three-quarters of the sauce, starting with the eggplant.

Top with the remaining sauce and the Parmesan cheese.

Cover the pot and place in a cold oven.

Set the temperature at 450 degrees.

Cook for 45 minutes.

MIDDLE EASTERN STUFFED PEPPERS

(SERVES 6)

SAUCE:

- 4 large ripe tomatoes, chopped coarsely
- 2 large onions, chopped fine
- ¼ cup water
- 1 teaspoon salt
- ½ teaspoon freshly ground pepper
- 1 teaspoon dried oregano
- 1 cup pinto beans (preferably fresh, but canned will do)

PEPPERS AND STUFFING:

- 6 green peppers
- 1 pound ground lamb
- 2 tablespoons chopped fresh mint or 1 tablespoon dried mint
- 1 clove garlic, crushed
- 1 small onion, chopped fine
- ½ teaspoon fresh grated nutmeg
- ½ teaspoon ground allspice
- 2 teaspoons salt
- ½ teaspoon freshly ground pepper
- ¾ cup slightly undercooked rice

Presoak a clay pot, top and bottom, in water for 15 minutes. Place all the ingredients for the sauce—except the pinto beans—into a saucepan and bring to a boil. Reduce the heat, cover the pan, and simmer slowly for 20 minutes.

Meanwhile, remove the tops of the peppers and take out the seeds and white pulp.

Mix all the ingredients for the stuffing, and stuff the peppers.

Place the stuffed peppers in the pot, pour the sauce over, and add the pinto beans.

Place the covered pot in a cold oven.

Turn the temperature to 450 degrees.

Cook for 50 to 60 minutes, testing the beans for doneness.

STUFFED GREEN PEPPERS

(SERVES 4)

4 *green peppers*
¼ *pound lean pork sausage*
½ *pound ground lean beef*
3 *tablespoons finely chopped fresh basil or 1 tablespoon*
   dried basil
3 *tablespoons finely chopped fresh sage or 1 tablespoon*
   dried sage
3 *soda crackers, crushed*
¼ *cup pine nuts*
1 *clove garlic, crushed*
1 *small onion, minced*
1 *egg*
1 *teaspoon arrowroot, approximately*

Presoak a clay pot, top and bottom, in water for 15 minutes.
Top the peppers, then remove the seeds and whitish pulp.
   Combine all the remaining ingredients, except the arrow-
   root, and stuff the peppers. Place the stuffed peppers in
   the pot.
Cover the pot and place it in a cold oven.
Set the oven temperature at 480 degrees.
Cook for 50 minutes, then remove the pot from the oven
   and pour off the liquid into a saucepan. Skim off the fat
   and bring to a boil, then thicken with arrowroot.

Classic Ethnic Dishes

VALENCIAN PAELLA

The classic dish of Spain (pronounced *pie-A-ya*) goes with green salad, garlic French bread, and, of course, wine, although you might try a good amber beer like the superb Mexican Dos Equis, but not too cold, or the local Steam Beer* if available.

2 *onions, chopped coarsely*
6 *large mushrooms, sliced thin*
1 *green pepper, chopped coarsely*
2 *cloves garlic, crushed*
½ *cup olive oil*
1 *frying chicken, cut into serving pieces*
Salt and freshly ground pepper
4 *hot Spanish sausages*
1½ *cups chicken broth*
1 *teaspoon paprika*
1 *teaspoon dried basil*
½ *teaspoon dried oregano*

* Steam Beer, a naturally carbonated brew (like champagne) was born during the Gold Rush, when San Francisco's temperate clime made it possible to brew a special beer without ice. One of the very few American beers worthy of the name, it is now available in bottles on the West Coast.

½ teaspoon saffron
¼ cup hot water
1½ cups raw rice
2 large tomatoes, quartered
2 sliced canned pimentoes
2 tablespoons capers
1 pound raw prawns, shelled and deveined
1 small can artichoke hearts
1 cup very hot clam broth
1 pound clams in their shells

Presoak a clay pot, top and bottom, in water for 15 minutes.

Sauté the onions, mushrooms, green pepper, and garlic in the olive oil until the onions turn golden brown, then remove from the oil and set aside. In the same frying pan, brown the chicken parts on all sides. Sprinkle with salt and pepper and set aside, then brown the cut-up sausage and set aside.

Add the chicken broth to the frying pan, bring to a boil, and add the paprika, basil, oregano, and saffron (diluted in ¼ cup hot water and crushed in a mortar). When the boiling point is reached, add the rice, stir, and simmer for 5 minutes.

Add the onion-mushroom-pepper mixture, tomatoes, 2 teaspoons salt, and 2 teaspoons pepper, then place in the bottom of the pot. Add the sausages, pimento, capers, prawns, and artichoke hearts and mix well, then top with the chicken parts and the very hot clam broth.

Cover the pot and place it in a cold oven.

Set the oven temperature at 480 degrees.

Cook for 35 minutes. Meanwhile, scrub the clams thoroughly under cold running water.

When the 35 minutes is up, remove the pot from the oven and add the clams. Return the covered pot to the oven and cook an additional 15 minutes.

STUFFED GRAPE LEAVES
(DOLMAS)

(SERVES 4)

¼ *pound ground lamb*
¼ *pound ground beef*
¼ *pound kefalotiri cheese or firm goat cheese, grated*
1 *onion, chopped fine*
1 *teaspoon sesame seeds*
½ *teaspoon dried oregano*
¼ *teaspoon dried marjoram*
¼ *teaspoon dried thyme*
3 *fresh mint leaves, crushed*
½ *cup cooked rice*
2 *cloves garlic, crushed*
1½ *teaspoons salt*
½ *teaspoon freshly ground pepper*
1 *sixteen-ounce jar grape leaves (available at Greek markets)*
½ *cup beef bouillon*
3 *tablespoons olive oil*

Presoak a clay pot, top and bottom, in water for 15 minutes.

Combine the ground lamb, ground beef, cheese, onion, sesame seeds, herbs, rice, garlic, salt, and pepper. Put a large tablespoonful of the mixture in center of each grape leaf, then turn the ends of the leaf in and roll it to fully enclose the filling.

Place the stuffed grape leaves in the presoaked pot, then combine the beef bouillon and olive oil and pour in.

Cover the pot and place it in a cold oven.
Set the oven temperature at 480 degrees.
Cook for 55 minutes.

LASAGNE

(SERVES 4 TO 6)

This meal-in-itself is made in two stages: first the sauce, then the lasagne.

SAUCE:

1 *pound lean ground beef*
6 *large mushrooms, sliced*
1 *large onion, chopped*
1 *tablespoon olive oil*
2 *tablespoons butter*
2 *eight-ounce cans tomato sauce*
Equal amount of water
¼ *cup dry white vermouth*
¼ *cup pine nuts*
3 *cloves garlic, crushed*
2 *tablespoons Marsala or Madeira*
2 *teaspoons salt*
1 *teaspoon freshly ground pepper*
1½ *teaspoons dried oregano*
1 *tablespoon dried basil*
⅓ *cup chopped ripe olives*

LASAGNE:

½ *pound "curly edge" lasagne*
Olive oil
½ *pint ricotta cheese (or dry cottage cheese)*
½ *pound* sharp *Cheddar cheese, grated*

1 cup sour cream

½ cup freshly grated Parmesan cheese

Start with the sauce. In a large frying pan, sauté the ground beef in the olive oil until it loses its raw, red color, then remove and set aside. In the same pan, sauté the sliced mushrooms and chopped onion in the butter until transparent. Return the beef to the frying pan, add all the other sauce ingredients, and cover. Simmer for 20 minutes.

Meanwhile, prepare the lasagne.

Presoak your largest clay pot, top and bottom, in water for 15 minutes.

Boil the lasagne according to directions on package, or as you would macaroni al dente, then drain and set aside.

Line the presoaked pot with a coating of olive oil, then add alternate layers of lasagne, sauce, mixed ricotta and Cheddar, and sour cream. When all these ingredients have been used up, sprinkle the top with the Parmesan cheese.

Cover the pot and place it in a cold oven.

Set the oven temperature at 480 degrees.

Cook for 45 minutes, or until done.

BETH COFFELT'S RICE PILAF

(SERVES 4 AS A SIDE DISH)

A Bay Area art critic, Beth Coffelt is also a grimly ferocious chess player. Her lair is Sausalito's famed No Name Bar, a hangout for artists, writers and serious chess buffs. Since she has been known to humiliate some insufferably smug male players after half a dozen moves, Ms. Coffelt has become one of the minor deities of local Women's Lib. It is no longer proper to call her a "master chef," while Mistress Cook sounds like Shakespearean comedy. Whatever—Beth Coffelt's rice pilaf steamed in the wet-pot is incontestably correct.

> 2 *tablespoons olive oil*
> 1 *onion, chopped*
> 1 *clove garlic, crushed*
> 1 *green pepper, chopped*
> 2 *tomatoes, chopped*
> 1 *cup raw long grain rice*
> *Pinch of saffron*
> 2 *cups chicken stock*
> ⅓ *cup pine nuts*
> ⅓ *cup currants or white raisins*
> 1 *teaspoon salt*
> *Pinch of freshly ground pepper*

Presoak a clay pot, top and bottom, in water for 15 minutes. In a saucepan, sauté the chopped onion, peppers, and garlic in the olive oil until transparent and tender. Add the tomatoes and set aside.

Add the saffron to the chicken stock and place it in the pre-soaked pot. Add the rice and stir, then add the pine nuts, currants or raisins, salt, pepper and the sautéed vegetable mixture. Stir thoroughly.

Cover the pot and place it in a cold oven.

Set the oven temperature at 480 degrees.

Cook for 45 minutes, or until the rice is tender.

LAMB-STUFFED CABBAGE LEAVES
(KOLDOLMA)

(SERVES 4)

Louis de Gouy, to our surprise, calls this a "traditional Swedish dish, borrowed from the Russians, who in turn got it from the Turks, whence its name, *Koldolma*, meaning 'cabbage cloaks.'" It cooks especially well in the small French "poulet form" clay pot, and makes an exquisite sauce.

12 to 16 large cabbage leaves (1 or 2 heads)
Salt
1 cup ground lamb
1 cup ground beef
1 medium onion, grated
¼ teaspoon grated nutmeg
2½ teaspoons salt
¼ teaspoon freshly ground black pepper
1 cup whole-wheat bread crumbs, moistened in olive oil
¼ cup dark molasses
¼ cup red wine
1 tablespoon olive oil
1 teaspoon arrowroot, approximately

Presoak a clay pot, top and bottom, in water for 15 minutes.

Remove 12 to 16 large leaves from the head(s) of cabbage. Steam them in ½ cup salted water for 3 to 4 minutes. Drain and set aside.

Chop enough of the remaining cabbage to make 1 cup and

combine with all the other ingredients except the molasses, wine, oil, and arrowroot. Place a heaping tablespoon of the mixture in center of each cabbage leaf, roll up, and place in the presoaked pot.

Combine the molasses, wine, and olive oil and pour over the stuffed cabbage leaves.

Cover the pot and place in a cold oven.

Set the oven temperature at 480 degrees.

Cook for 70 minutes.

When done, remove the pot from the oven and pour off the sauce into a saucepan. Bring it to a boil and thicken with the arrowroot mixed with a little water. Pour over the cabbage rolls and serve.

Note: You can use 2 cups ground lamb and omit the beef, if preferred.

CASSOULET
(SOUTHERN FRENCH COUNTRY COOKING)
(SERVES 6)

Cassoulet, the hearty traditional beans-with-meat dish of provincial France, is subject to much variation and endless Gallic dispute like the recipes for Boston baked beans, a "true" clam chowder, or the pemmican of the American Indians. Some, for example, insist that goose is essential. Feel free to experiment, but the important thing is not to hurry the dish, a meal-in-itself aromatic delight that often takes three days of leisurely country cooking in France. Our adaptation for the clay pot is somewhat condensed, but no less succulent.

  1 *pound ham hocks*
  1 *pound white pea beans (soaked overnight)*
  ½ *ten-and-one-half-ounce can beef consommé, more if necessary*
  1 *cup tomato juice*
  2 *large onions, each stuck with 4 cloves*
  4 *whole cloves garlic, peeled*
  2 *bay leaves*
  1 *teaspoon dried thyme*
  1 *pound boneless lamb or chicken, cubed*
  3 *to 4 hot Spanish sausages, cut up*
  1 *pound boneless pork, cubed*
  3 *tablespoons bacon fat*
  Salt and freshly ground pepper
  2 *large onions, chopped fine*

Place the ham hocks, pea beans, consommé, tomato juice, whole onions, garlic, bay leaves, and thyme in a large saucepan. Add enough water to cover by ½ inch and bring to a boil. Turn the flame as low as possible, *cover*, and barely simmer for 5 hours; add more water if necessary.

When the 5 hours are about up, presoak a large clay pot, top and bottom, in water for 15 minutes.

In a frying pan, brown the lamb, sausage, and pork in the bacon fat. Add salt and pepper to taste, then place in the presoaked pot. In the same frying pan, brown the chopped onions in the meat drippings, then add to the meat in the pot, along with the ham hock–bean mixture. (The combination should be soupy; you may have to add a small amount of consommé.)

Cover the pot and place in a cold oven.

Set the oven temperature at 450 degrees.

Cook for 1 hour.

LAMB CURRY

(SERVES 4)

With a bit of care about the key ingredients, this gives you a matchless curry.

Ask your butcher for boneless rolled shoulder of lamb, cheaper than most other cuts. When trimmed of fat, cut into bite-sized pieces, and steamed in the wet-pot, this inexpensive lamb gets buttery-tender. You need a first-rate curry powder, imported from India; the Maharaja brand from Madras gives superlative results. You'll have to experiment with the quantity, but Maharaja curry used in the proportions given below strikes the right balance between blandness and scalp-remover hot. The recipe calls for Maggi seasoning, a good condiment to have around, adding a meaty taste when used with discretion; beef bouillon may be substituted, though we prefer Maggi.

3 pounds rolled boneless shoulder of lamb, trimmed of fat
2 large yellow onions, minced fine
¾ cup shredded coconut
2 cloves garlic, crushed
1 tablespoon grated fresh ginger
½ cup red wine
1 teaspoon Maggi seasoning
2½ tablespoons good-quality Madras curry powder
1 teaspoon salt
1 teaspoon arrowroot, approximately

Presoak a clay pot, top and bottom, in water for 15 minutes.

Cut the lamb into bite-sized pieces, then combine with all the other ingredients, except the arrowroot, and place in the presoaked pot.

Cover the pot and place it in a cold oven.

Set the oven temperature at 400 degrees.

Cook for 90 minutes, then remove the pot from the oven and pour off the liquid into a saucepan. Heat and add 1 teaspoon or more arrowroot to thicken.

Pour the thickened sauce back into the pot, and serve over brown rice with a curry condiment tray including sufficient portions of:

Chopped hard-boiled egg

Chopped nuts (peanuts or cashews)

Chopped scallions or chives

Black currants

Shredded coconut

Chutneys (both a bland raisin chutney and a strong mango chutney—clearly marked)

Chopped dill pickle

Mandarin oranges

Diced fresh pineapple

ATHENIAN MOUSSAKA

(SERVES 4)

1½ cups finely chopped meat (ham, salami, hamburger,
    in any desired proportions)
½ pint ricotta cheese
½ pint cottage cheese
¼ cup chopped fresh mint leaves
¼ cup chopped fresh parsley
½ cup chopped green onions
2 tablespoons chopped chives
3 ounces (1-pint carton) alfalfa sprouts
½ pound grated Monterey Jack cheese

COMBINE:

3 eggs, well beaten
¼ teaspoon dried basil
¼ teaspoon dried oregano
¼ teaspoon freshly ground pepper
1 teaspoon good-quality Indian curry powder
1 teaspoon salt, more or less, according to the amount
    of salami or ham used

Presoak a small clay pot, top and bottom, in water for 15
minutes.

Place alternate layers of the meat, cottage cheese, ricotta,
mint, parsley, green onions, chives, alfalfa sprouts, and
Monterey Jack cheese in the presoaked pot. Combine the
remaining ingredients and add.

Cover the pot and place it in a cold oven.
Set the oven temperature at 450 degrees.
Cook for 35 minutes.

CHINESE SWEET-AND-SOUR SPARERIBS

(SERVES 4 TO 5)

This traditional Chinese recipe, served with its renowned sauce that can enhance a variety of dishes, is easily adapted to the pot. It proved to be one of our most successful experiments, and you'll find yourself going back to it again and again.

Ask your butcher for "country-style" spareribs, so much meatier than the usual kind. Sesame oil, used in small quantities as much for its aroma as its taste, is standard for the finishing touch of many Chinese dishes.

SWEET-AND-SOUR SAUCE:

  1 *cup malt vinegar, more if necessary*
  2 *tablespoons salt, more if necessary*
  1 *cup granulated sugar, more if necessary*
  ½ *cup orange juice*
  ½ *cup pineapple juice*
  ½ *cup tomato paste*
  Arrowroot

SPARERIBS:

  4 *pounds country-style spareribs, trimmed of all fat*
  3 *teaspoons salt*
  ½ *teaspoon freshly ground pepper*
  6 *small white onions, peeled and quartered*
  1 *green pepper, cut into bite-sized chunks*
  2 *very firm medium-sized tomatoes, quartered*

10 pineapple chunks, preferably fresh
Arrowroot
Dash of sesame oil

Combine all the ingredients for the sauce, except the arrowroot, in a saucepan. Bring to a slow boil, cover, and simmer gently for 10 minutes. Taste the sauce to determine the proper balance of saltiness, sweetness, and sourness. (Use more salt if necessary; if too sweet, add malt vinegar *slowly*. If too sour, add a bit of sugar.) Thicken the sauce by bringing to a low boil and adding enough arrowroot (mixed with a little water) to make the consistency heavy.

Presoak a large clay pot, top and bottom, in water for 10 minutes.

Rub the spareribs with 2 teaspoons of the salt and the pepper. With a pastry brush, paint all sides of meat generously with the sauce, then place the ribs in the presoaked pot.

Cover the pot and place it in a cold oven.

Set the oven temperature at 480 degrees.

Cook for 55 minutes.

Meanwhile, because they must be added quickly, place the onions, pepper, tomatoes, and pineapple chunks on a large plate. When the ribs have cooked 55 minutes, remove the pot from the oven, uncover, and *quickly* add the fruit and vegetables from the plate. Sprinkle with the remaining salt and top with a generous dollop of the sweet-and-sour sauce.

Return the covered pot to the oven and cook for an additional 25 minutes (total cooking time: about 80 minutes).

Remove the pot from the oven and pour off the sauce into

a saucepan, heat, and thicken with arrowroot. Mix some more sweet-and-sour sauce with this and pour over the spareribs.

Sprinkle a few drops of sesame oil over the dish, stir lightly, and serve.

Note: Any sauce left over can be stored and used again for barbecuing and for many other types of cooking. Pour the sauce into a large-mouthed jar and cover with waxed paper and rubber bands. Don't cover tightly or the gases formed by the salt-vinegar combination can't escape.

GREEK LASAGNE

(SERVES 4)

This Greek variation uses the homemade green lasagne that gets its color from spinach. It should be available in any of the Italian or Greek import specialty markets. There's really no comparison between most packaged lasagne and the homemade kind. The cheese given in the recipe below may be varied to suit your taste.

¾ *pound green lasagne*

1 *pound ground beef*

2 *hard-boiled eggs, chopped*

8 *grape leaves, chopped coarsely*

2 *cloves garlic, minced*

1½ *teaspoons salt*

¼ *pound sharp Cheddar cheese, sliced*

¼ *pound Monterey Jack cheese, sliced*

2 *ounces Camembert cheese, sliced*

¼ *cup freshly grated Parmesan cheese*

1 *tablespoon finely chopped fresh basil or 1 teaspoon dried basil*

1 *medium-sized can solid-pack tomatoes, drained*

1 *tablespoon olive oil*

Presoak a large unglazed clay pot, top and bottom, in water for 15 minutes.

Brown the ground beef in a frying pan, then discard any fat. Pour the olive oil into the presoaked pot, add a layer of lasagne, and alternate all the other ingredients except

the Parmesan cheese, ending with a layer of lasagne.
Sprinkle the top with the Parmesan.

Cover the pot and put it in a cold oven.

Set the oven temperature at 480 degrees.

Cook for 45 minutes, removing the lid the last five minutes
to brown.

FLEMISH LAMB AND OYSTER PIE

(SERVES 4)

This Flemish variation on the traditional English beef and kidney pie is well worth the little extra trouble which isn't nearly as much as it seems.

FLOUR MIXTURE:

¼ cup all-purpose flour

1 teaspoon salt

Pinch of freshly ground pepper

⅛ teaspoon dried thyme

⅛ teaspoon dried sage

⅛ teaspoon marjoram

⅛ teaspoon ground mace

2 pounds boneless lamb stew meat, cut into small cubes

1 tablespoon butter

2 tablespoons lard or chicken fat

6 leeks, cleaned and cut into 2-inch lengths

6 carrots, peeled and sliced into very thin rounds

6 large mushrooms, sliced thin

1 ten-and-one-half-ounce can beef bouillon

1 onion, chopped fine

1 clove garlic, minced

12 oysters, shucked

1 cup freshly shelled peas or 1 ten-ounce package frozen peas

¼ cup chopped fresh parsley or 1 tablespoon dried parsley

Pastry crust for a one-crust pie

Presoak a clay pot, top and bottom, in water for 15 minutes.

Combine the flour, salt, pepper, and herbs in a paper bag and mix thoroughly. Add the cubed lamb and shake. Set aside any remaining flour mixture.

In a frying pan, brown the lamb well on all sides in the butter and lard, then put in the presoaked pot. Put the leeks, carrots, and mushrooms in the frying pan along with the bouillon, and simmer for 5 minutes. Remove the vegetables with a slotted spoon and add to the pot, leaving the bouillon in the pan. Flour the chopped onion and garlic in the remaining flour mixture, add to the bouillon, and simmer until thickened.

Meanwhile, add the oysters and peas to the pot and mix the contents gently. Pour the bouillon mixture into the pot, add the chopped parsley, then cover the contents of the pot with the pastry crust (your own favorite recipe); slash the crust in several places to allow steam to escape.

Cover the pot and place it in a cold oven.

Set the oven temperature at 480 degrees.

Cook for 50 minutes.

Remove the lid for the last 5 minutes to brown the crust.

Serve right from the pot.

BEEF BOURGUIGNONNE

(SERVES 4)

This traditional French casserole dish lends itself admirably to the clay pot, particularly the small French "poulet form."

2½ pounds round of beef, cut into 1-inch cubes

MARINADE:

½ cup brandy
½ cup red wine

FLOUR MIXTURE:

¼ cup all-purpose flour
1 teaspoon salt
¼ teaspoon freshly ground pepper

½ cup diced bacon
2 cups beef bouillon
12 tiny white onions, peeled
8 small carrots, peeled and cut in half lengthwise
6 large mushrooms, sliced
2 cloves garlic, crushed
¼ cup chopped fresh parsley
2 bay leaves
1 tablespoon tomato paste
½ teaspoon dried thyme
½ teaspoon salt
1 teaspoon arrowroot (optional)

Marinate the cubed beef overnight in ½ cup each brandy and red wine. When ready to cook, drain the beef and reserve the marinade.

Presoak a clay pot, top and bottom, in water for 15 minutes.

Combine the flour, 1 teaspoon salt, and the pepper in a paper bag, add the beef, and shake. Set aside any remaining flour mixture.

In frying pan, cook the diced bacon in olive oil until lightly browned, then remove with a slotted spoon and set aside on a paper towel to drain. Sauté the floured beef in the remaining bacon fat and olive oil until browned on all sides, then pour off most of the fat, add ½ cup of the bouillon, and simmer for 10 minutes. Remove the beef cubes from the pan with a slotted spoon, reflour in the remaining flour mix, and place in the presoaked pot, along with the small white onions, carrots, and mushrooms.

To the drippings in the frying pan, add the crushed garlic, chopped parsley, bay leaves, tomato paste, thyme, remaining salt, and reserved marinade (combined with enough equal amounts of brandy and wine to make 1 cup). Mix well and pour into the clay pot.

Cover the pot and place it in a cold oven.

Set the oven temperature at 450 degrees.

Cook for 1 hour.

Then remove the pot from the oven and add the bacon cracklings.

Test the sauce for thickness and the meat for doneness. (If the sauce is too thick, add *heated* wine, being careful not to pour it directly on the hot clay; if the sauce is too thin, pour it off into a saucepan. Skim off the fat, heat it, and thicken with arrowroot, then adjust seasoning to taste and pour back into the pot.)

Serve with plain boiled potatoes for a traditional bourguignon dinner—or, if you prefer, boiled noodles.

HASENPFEFFER
(OLD-STYLE GERMAN RABBIT)

(SERVES 4)

This classic rabbit dish from the old country needs half a week to marinate, but it's worth the trouble.

1 rabbit, skinned and cut into serving pieces, blood and liver reserved

MARINADE:
- *¾ cup white wine*
- *¾ cup water*
- *1 onion, sliced*
- *1 carrot, sliced*
- *2 bay leaves*
- *1 tablespoon fresh thyme or 1 teaspoon dried thyme*
- *1 teaspoon whole peppercorns*

FLOUR MIXTURE:
- *3 tablespoons all-purpose flour*
- *1 teaspoon salt*
- *Pinch of freshly ground pepper*

- *2 tablespoons bacon fat*
- *8 small white onions*
- *12 mushroom caps*
- *¼ cup white wine*
- *½ cup minced fresh parsley*
- *2 bay leaves*

1 tablespoon fresh thyme or ½ tablespoon dried thyme
1 cup sour cream

In a large glass or crockery bowl (*no* metal), combine ¾ cup of the white wine, the water, onion, carrot, half the bay leaves, half the thyme, the peppercorns, and the blood and liver of the rabbit. Add the rabbit and marinate for 3 to 5 days in a cool spot.

When ready to cook, presoak an unglazed clay pot, top and bottom, in water for 15 minutes.

Remove the rabbit from the marinade and dry with paper towels. Reserve the marinade. Put the flour, salt, and pepper in a paper bag, add the rabbit, and shake to coat the pieces. Save any remaining flour mixture.

Brown the rabbit in the bacon fat, then place in the presoaked pot, along with the small white onions, mushroom caps, and the rabbit liver, which has been chopped and lightly browned.

Strain the reserved marinade and boil it down to 1 cup of liquid. Add the remaining ¼ cup white wine mixed with the remaining flour mixture, cook until thickened, and pour into the pot. Add the minced parsley, remaining 2 bay leaves, and remaining thyme.

Cover the pot and place it in a cold oven.

Set the oven temperature at 450 degrees.

Cook for 55 minutes.

Test for doneness, then remove the meat to a platter.

Thicken the sauce with the sour cream and pour over the rabbit.

Serve with boiled new potatoes or egg noodles.

MIDDLE EASTERN EGGPLANT

(SERVES 2)

Ancients believed the eggplant—like the tomato—to be poisonous, and many Americans still harbor a subliminal aversion to this noble fruit-vegetable that remains a mainstay of Middle Eastern cooking. As the cuisine of Armenia, Greece, and Turkey grows increasingly popular in our large urban centers, the eggplant promises to be rescued from semi-obscurity.

In his superb *Gold Cook Book**—a "must" for every kitchen shelf—Louis De Gouy tells us to "select eggplant by its weight, the heavier the better. Be sure the outside skin is intact or it will impair the flavor." De Gouy, who offers seasoned advice about the selection, purchase, and preparation of everything edible, assures us that the old wives' tale about soaking eggplant in salt water before cooking is just that—and besides it "draws out some of the nutritive value and flavor."

1 *large eggplant*
¼ *pound lean ground lamb*
2 *tablespoons butter*
1 *tablespoon chopped canned pimento*
½ *cup chopped onion*
1 *clove garlic, crushed*
3 *soda crackers, crumbled*
⅛ *cup pine nuts*

* Greenberg: Publisher, 1947.

¼ teaspoon salt
Pinch of freshly ground pepper

Presoak a clay pot, top and bottom, in water for 15 minutes.

Cut the eggplant in half. Carefully remove the pulp and chop it fine. Set the skins aside.

Heat the butter in a frying pan, add the chopped onion, and cook to a light golden brown. Add the ground lamb, finely chopped eggplant, and crushed garlic and cook until the eggplant is slightly transparent. Remove from heat and add pimento, cracker crumbs, pine nuts, salt, and pepper. Fill the reserved eggplant skins with this mixture and place in the presoaked pot.

Cover the pot and place it in a cold oven.

Set the oven temperature at 450 degrees.

Cook for 40 minutes.

OLD MUNICH SAUERBRATEN

(SERVES 6)

This sturdy delight formed the backbone of one of our most memorable dinner parties. We served it with potato pancakes, homemade apple sauce, sweet and sour red cabbage, and apple strudel, giving our guests the choice of Dos Equis, Mexico's magnificent amber beer, or Charles Krug's Zinfandel (uncorked a few hours before serving). Some guests had both! The trick is to marinate the meat a *long* time, at least 10 days, and turn it twice daily. The sauce that emerges from the pot after cooking is something your guests will be talking about for days.

MARINADE:

1 *cup vinegar, more if necessary*
1 *cup water*
10 *whole cloves*
Bouquet garni of 4 bay leaves, 2 sprigs celery leaves, and 1 sprig fresh thyme
3 *juniper berries, crushed*
1 *large onion, sliced thin*
3 *cloves garlic, crushed*
2 *teaspoons salt*
1 *whole lemon, sliced*

MEAT:

1 *bottom round roast of beef (about 5 pounds)*
2 *tablespoons bacon fat*
1 *eight-ounce can tomato sauce*

1 *bouillon cube*

½ *cup red wine*

3 *tablespoons brown sugar, more if necessary*

3 *to 4 strips lemon peel*

5 *gingersnaps, crumbled*

1 *tablespoon Worcestershire sauce*

1½ *teaspoons arrowroot, approximately*

Combine all the ingredients for the marinade in a porcelain-enameled container. Add the meat and for best results marinate for 10 days, if not more. Turn twice daily.

When ready to cook, presoak a large clay pot, top and bottom, in water for 15 minutes.

Remove the meat from marinade, put in a large frying pan, and sear on all sides in the hot bacon fat. Meanwhile, pour the marinade into a saucepan and reduce to ⅓ its original volume by boiling rapidly, uncovered. Place the meat in the presoaked pot, then add the marinade and all the other ingredients except the arrowroot.

Cover the pot and place it in a cold oven.

Set the oven temperature at 425 degrees.

Cook for 2 to 2½ hours, until almost done, then remove the pot from the oven and pour off the sauce. Return the pot to the oven, uncovered, for a final 10 minutes of cooking.

Meanwhile, put the sauce into a blender container and blend.

Taste for seasoning; the sauce should be "sweet and sour." If not, add brown sugar and/or vinegar. Heat the sauce, thicken with the arrowroot, and serve over the meat and German potato pancakes (page 85).

Chowders & Soups

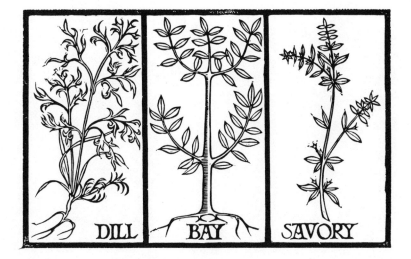

DILL   BAY   SAVORY

The formidable Louis De Gouy tells us the word "chowder" comes from the French for cauldron; *la chaudière,* or "hotpot." A sort of gourmet Mulligan Stew, the French chowder was often a community pastiche at festival time, when many families made their contribution to the pot. De Gouy cautions that, despite Ladies' Tea Shoppe debasements, the three indispensable ingredients are clams, onions and salt pork—or in this case, bacon. Those who like tomatoes in their clam chowder are urged to consult some other cookbook.

BOSTON CLAM CHOWDER

(SERVES 2 AS A MAIN COURSE, 4 AS A SOUP COURSE)

- 2 *dozen clams in the shells or 3 seven-ounce cans diced clams plus 1 can clam nectar*
- 1 *cup water*
- 1 *clove garlic, crushed*
- 3 *slices bacon, chopped*
- 2 *large onions, chopped*
- ½ *cup finely chopped fresh parsley*
- 2 *medium potatoes, peeled and diced*
- 2 *bay leaves*

1   *quart whole milk or half-and-half*
2   *tablespoons all-purpose flour*
2   *tablespoons butter*
Salt and freshly ground pepper
1   *teaspoon Worcestershire sauce*
Dash of Tabasco sauce

Presoak a clay pot, top and bottom, in water for 15 minutes.
Scrub the clams in their shells under cold running water,
    then place in a covered saucepan with 1 cup of the water
    and the crushed garlic. Heat slowly until the clams open,
    then remove from the pan and discard the shells. Coarsely
    chop *half* of the clams and leave the remainder whole.
    Pour all the clams and the nectar into the presoaked pot.
Lightly brown the bacon in a frying pan. Add the bacon to
    the pot, but leave the fat in the frying pan. To the bacon
    fat in the pan, add the chopped onion and cook to a golden
    brown. Add the parsley for a few minutes, then put the
    mixture in the clay pot. Simmer the diced potatoes in ½
    cup water with salt and pepper until just tender, then
    add both potatoes and cooking liquid to the pot. Add the
    milk (or half-and-half). Knead the butter and flour into
    a ball and add to the pot, along with salt and pepper to
    taste.
Cover the pot and place it in a cold oven.
Set the oven temperature at 450 degrees.
Cook for 40 minutes.
Remove the pot from the oven and add Worcestershire
    sauce and Tabasco, and more salt and pepper, if desired.

GROUND MUSHROOM SOUP

(SERVES 4)

Here's a lunch in itself: not the usual thin, delicate mushroom soup, but a thick, gusty stew. Steaming the ground mushrooms in the wet-pot wrings a unique flavor from the noble fungi.

>   1 *pound fresh mushrooms*
>   1 *large onion*
>   2 *tablespoons butter*
>   2 *tablespoons all-purpose flour*
>   1 *quart whole milk or half-and-half*
>   1 *small clove garlic, crushed*
>   2 *bay leaves*
>   1 *teaspoon salt*
>   ½ *teaspoon freshly ground pepper*
>   2 *egg yolks, beaten*
>   *Pinch of cayenne*
>   1 *pint heavy cream*
>   *Freshly grated Parmesan cheese*

Presoak a medium-sized or large clay pot, top and bottom, in water for 15 minutes.

Grind the mushrooms and onion fine in a meat grinder, then place in a saucepan, add the butter, and simmer for 5 minutes. Add the flour, blend well, and pour into the presoaked pot. In a bowl, combine the milk, garlic, bay leaves, salt, and pepper, and pour into the pot.

Cover the pot and place it in a cold oven.

Set the oven temperature at 450 degrees.

Cook for 45 minutes, then remove from the oven and add the egg yolks, cayenne, and heavy cream. Stir briskly.

Serve with the Parmesan cheese.

OXTAIL SOUP

(SERVES 2 AS A MAIN COURSE, 4 AS A SOUP COURSE)

> 2 tablespoons all-purpose flour
> 1 medium oxtail (1½ to 2 pounds)
> 2 onions, chopped
> 4 stalks celery, sliced
> 1 green pepper, chopped fine
> 3 carrots, peeled and sliced thin
> 6 large mushrooms, sliced thin
> 2 ripe tomatoes, chopped
> 2 teaspoons salt
> ½ teaspoon freshly ground pepper
> 1 clove garlic, crushed
> 1½ quarts water
> 2 beef bouillon cubes
> 2 bay leaves
> 1 teaspoon dried thyme
> 2 tablespoons bacon fat

Presoak a clay pot, top and bottom, in water for 15 minutes.
Flour the oxtail, brown in the bacon fat and place in the pre-
   soaked pot. Add all the other ingredients.
Cover the pot and place it in a cold oven.
Set the oven temperature at 425 degrees.
Cook for 1½ to 2 hours.

CREAM OF PUMPKIN SOUP

(SERVES 4)

"This must have taken you *hours* to make!" is the comment from guests once they've tasted this elegant soup. Short of opening a can, we don't know of a soup easier or quicker to make.

1 *medium onion, quartered*
1 *quart chicken stock*
1 *one-pound can of pumpkin or 2 cups fresh pumpkin*
1½ *teaspoons good-quality Madras curry powder*
1 *tablespoon Worcestershire sauce*
Salt and freshly ground pepper
½ *pint whipping cream, scalded*
½ *pint sour cream*

Presoak a clay pot, top and bottom, for 15 minutes.
Put the quartered onion and a small amount of the chicken stock in a blender container, blend, and pour into the presoaked pot. Add the remainder of the chicken stock, the pumpkin, curry powder, and Worcestershire sauce and mix thoroughly. Add salt and pepper to taste.
Cover the pot and place it in a cold oven.
Set the oven temperature at 450 degrees.
Cook for 35 minutes, then remove from the oven and add the scalded whipping cream. Stir well, pour into bowls and top with the sour cream.

ARMENIAN LENTIL SOUP WITH HAM HOCKS
(SERVES 2 TO 4)

Like many thick soups, this 3,500-year-old staple of Arabia and North Africa improves when warmed over and eaten the next day—if it lasts that long.

Ask the butcher to cut the ham hocks in half.

> 1 *cup dried lentils*
> 2 *ham hocks*
> 2 *large cloves garlic, crushed*
> 2 *large onions, chopped fine*
> ½ *cup chopped fresh parsley*
> 2 *teaspoons dried thyme*
> 2 *bay leaves*
> 1½ *quarts water*
> 1 *tablespoon salt*

Soak the lentils overnight in enough water to cover.

When ready to cook, presoak a clay pot for 15 minutes. Put the lentils in the presoaked clay pot, after draining off and discarding the water, then add the ham hocks and all the other ingredients.

Cover the pot and place in a cold oven.

Set the oven temperature at 450 degrees.

Cook for 1½ to 2 hours.

BLACK BEAN AND LAMB'S TONGUE SOUP
(FROM AFRICA)
(SERVES 2 AS A MAIN COURSE, 4 AS A SOUP COURSE)

1 cup black beans

4 teaspoons salt

1 cup water

4 to 5 lamb's tongues

½ teaspoon granulated sugar

2 lemons, sliced unpeeled

1½ quarts beef stock

1 teaspoon freshly ground black pepper

1 onion, chopped

½ teaspoon good-quality Madras curry powder

1 cup red wine

Soak the black beans overnight in enough water to cover, to
which 1 teaspoon salt has been added.

When ready to cook, presoak a clay pot, top and bottom, in
water for 15 minutes.

Drain off all the water from the beans: add the 1 cup water
and simmer until almost tender, then pour the beans and
cooking liquid into the pot. Add all the other ingredients.

Cover the pot and place it in a cold oven.

Set the oven temperature at 450 degrees.

Cook for 1 hour. Check for doneness. (You may want to add
more water.)

GERMAN PRUNE SOUP WITH DUMPLINGS
(SERVES 2 AS A MAIN COURSE, 4 AS A SOUP COURSE)

Georgia's grandmother, a fabulous Old World cook, gave her this unusual recipe, available neither in cans nor restaurants. Its characteristic German sweet-and-sour bite and aroma fulfills the prime purpose of a good soup: salivation to goad taste buds and the entire digestive process for the meal to follow.

SOUP:

>   1 *dozen dried prunes*
>   4 *slices thick-cut bacon, chopped*
>   1 *small onion, chopped fine*
>   ½ *cup granulated sugar*
>   ½ *cup* cider *vinegar*
>   ½ *teaspoon salt*
>   1½ *quarts water*

DUMPLINGS:

>   ½ *dry coffee cake or about 3 dry cinnamon rolls*
>   ¼ *cup all-purpose flour*
>   2 *tablespoons granulated sugar*
>   1 *tablespoon softened butter*
>   1 *egg, beaten slightly*
>   *Milk*

Presoak a clay pot, top and bottom, in water for 15 minutes. Place all the ingredients for the soup in the presoaked pot, then cover the pot and place it in a cold oven.

Set the oven temperature at 480 degrees.

Cook for 75 minutes.

While the soup is cooking prepare the dumplings: Combine the crumpled coffee cake, flour, and sugar, and mix well. Add the butter and egg and mix to make a soft dumpling-style dough. If not soft enough, add a little milk.

At the end of the cooking time, remove the soup from oven and drop the dumplings into the soup by the spoonful. (Make about 8 dumplings and you may have some left over.) Cover the pot and return it to the oven for an additional 20 minutes of cooking.

GERMAN GREEN BEAN SOUP

(SERVES 2 AS A MAIN COURSE, 4 AS A SOUP COURSE)

Here's another appetizer handed down by Georgia's German grandmother.

1 *pound green beans, frenched and cut in 3-inch lengths*
4 *slices thick-cut bacon, chopped*
1 *small onion, chopped fine*
¼ *cup all-purpose flour*
5 *cups water*
½ *cup granulated sugar*
½ *cup cider vinegar*

Presoak a clay pot, top and bottom, in water for 15 minutes.
Place the beans in the bottom of the presoaked pot. Cook the bacon and onion in a frying pan until golden, then pour over the beans. Clean the frying pan, sprinkle in the flour, and heat over a high flame until flour tans. Mix in 3 cups of the water to make a thickened sauce, then pour over the beans. Combine the remaining 2 cups water, the sugar, and vinegar, and pour over the beans.
Cover the pot and place it in a cold oven.
Set the oven temperature at 450 degrees.
Cook for 60 to 70 mintues.
Serve with a hearty bread and good stout beer.

Bread & Cake

B R E A D baking in the wet-pot was a belated and surprising discovery. When Georgia suggested it, my first reaction, which may well be yours, was "Why bother? What's the advantage of baking bread in the pot over ordinary oven baking?" Georgia found the answer in Julian Street's delightful collection of essays and recipes, *Table Topics.* * Perplexed by the inability of most American cooks to turn out a true French bread, Street consulted the chief baker of the Waldorf-Astoria during that institution's *Hotel Splendide* days circa World War I. "The principal things we learned were that for French bread *there must be steam in the oven* and that the addition of sugar to the dough helps to brown the crust. We believe the following recipe will produce as good a loaf as it is possible to make *in the ordinary American household range, with heat coming not evenly from all sides but from the bottom only . . .*"

The wet-pot, which manufactures its own steam, also ensures that the heat comes "evenly from all sides." Here, ready at hand, was a miniature replica of Julian Street's French oven. The genuine French loaf that emerged plump, moist, and golden brown from the pot soon convinced us to try a variety of breads and pastries, with smashing results. In homage to the late Julian Street, who suggested the way to a superior method of baking, we begin this section with his

* Alfred A. Knopf, Inc., 1959.

nonpareil French bread. Don't expect the rough, coarse texture of San Francisco's famous sourdough French bread, however; this bread has a finer, crumblier, down-home character all its own.

JULIAN STREET'S FRENCH BRICK-OVEN BREAD

½ *cup milk, scalded*
1¼ *cups water*
1½ *tablespoons vegetable shortening or lard*
1 *package active dry yeast or ½ ounce fresh yeast*
1½ *tablespoons granulated sugar*
4 *cups all-purpose flour*
2 *teaspoons salt*

Combine the scalded milk with 1 cup boiling water and cool to lukewarm, then add the shortening. Combine the yeast with the remaining ¼ cup water, warmed to lukewarm, and 1 tablespoon of the sugar. Set aside.

Combine the flour, salt and remaining sugar in a large mixing bowl and blend well. Add the lukewarm milk mixture to the yeast mixture, then pour into the flour. Stir thoroughly, but *don't* knead. (The dough will be soft.) Place the dough in a well-greased large bowl, cover with a damp cloth, and set aside in a warm place until it rises to double its bulk (about 1 hour). At the end of the rising time, divide the dough into 2 equal parts and form into long, thin rolls to fit the pot.

Presoak one or more clay pots, top and bottom, in water for 15 minutes.

Place a small piece of aluminum foil in the bottom of the pot to prevent sticking. Place the loaves in the pot or pots, cover with a lid, and allow to rise in a warm place to almost double its bulk.

Cover the pot(s) and place in a cold oven.

Set the oven temperature at 525 degrees.

Bake for 45 minutes, removing the lid for the last 5 minutes of baking to brown the crust.

HERB-OATMEAL BREAD

This unusual loaf is worth every second of the 3½ hours it takes from start to finish. Be sure you make enough of it, because it will put on a cookie-like disappearing act. Be careful about the ingredients, especially oatmeal; get a *good* one, like John McCann's from Ireland, and spurn the instant oatmeal as you would freeze-dried Chablis!

- 2 *packages active dry yeast or 1 ounce fresh yeast*
- 3 *tablespoons honey*
- 1½ *tablespoons salt*
- 2 *cups water*
- ¾ *cup oatmeal (not instant)*
- 2 *tablespoons sour cream or 1 cup light cream*
- ¾ *cup whole-wheat flour*
- 1 *teaspoon celery seeds*
- 1 *teaspoon poppy seeds*
- 1 *tablespoon sesame seeds*
- 1 *tablespoon fresh sage, chopped or 1 teaspoon dried sage*
- 1 *tablespoon fresh basil, chopped or 1 teaspoon dried basil*
- ½ *teaspoon dried dill*
- 1 *egg, beaten*
- 2 *tablespoons butter, melted*
- ½ *cup pine nuts*
- 4 *cups all-purpose flour*

Combine the yeast, honey, and salt with 1 cup *lukewarm*

(not hot) water and set aside. (Remember: if the water is too hot it will kill the growing yeast.)

Heat 1 cup water to boiling, and add the oatmeal and sour cream. Simmer, covered, for 10 minutes, then remove from the heat and cool to lukewarm. Combine the whole-wheat flour, seeds, and herbs in a large mixing bowl. Add the oatmeal and yeast mixtures and beat until well blended. Add beaten egg and melted butter and beat several times again. Add the pine nuts, then add 3 cups of the all-purpose flour, one cup at a time, beating between each addition until a fairly stiff dough is developed.

Spread the remaining all-purpose flour on a board and knead the dough into it thoroughly, about a dozen times, then put the dough in a large, well-greased bowl and cover with a damp cloth. Set to rise in a warm place until double its original bulk (about 1 hour).

Just before the end of the rising time, presoak 2 clay pots, top and bottom, in water for 15 minutes. (We use 2 pots in order to bake each loaf separately.)

Place the risen dough on a floured board, divide, and shape into 2 loaves. Before putting the loaves in the presoaked pots, put a small piece of aluminum foil, just large enough to cover the bottom of the loaf, on the bottom of each pot. (This keeps the bread from sticking to the pot.) Place the dough inside the pots, cover, and allow to rise until almost doubled in bulk (about 45 minutes).

Cover the pots and put them in a cold oven.

Set the oven temperature at 480 degrees.

Bake for 40 minutes. If necessary, remove the lid for the last 5 minutes of baking to get a golden brown crust.

MARYETTA'S ITALIAN SAUSAGE BREAD

Maryetta Moose, one of San Francisco's greatest cooks, gave us this meal-in-itself from the oven. Her recipe calls for freshly-made Italian sweet sausage, which she buys across the street from her North Beach apartment. If you suspect your sausage contains too much fat, see the instructions below. And while you're shopping for fresh Italian sausage, try to get fresh yeast from an Italian bakery.

> 1 *pound sweet Italian sausage*
> 1¼ *cups lukewarm water*
> 1 *teaspoon salt*
> 1 *package dry active yeast or ½ ounce fresh yeast*
> *Small pinch of saffron*
> 1 *tablespoon fennel seeds*
> 4 *cups sifted all-purpose flour*
> *Scant ⅛ cup olive oil*
> *Cornmeal*

If you think your sausage has too much fat, simmer in shallow water in a frying pan, pricking the sausage with a sharp knife to allow the fat to escape.

Combine the lukewarm water, salt, yeast, saffron, and fennel seeds in a metal cup and maintain a lukewarm temperature to keep the yeast active. Sift the flour into a large bowl, and make a well in the center of it. Pour in the yeast mixture and mix well (you will have to use your hands). Knead the dough until smooth and elastic (about 10 minutes), then pour the oil over the dough and knead until no longer sticky (about 5 minutes). Place in a large bowl, cover with a towel, and put in a warm place until it doubles in size. (Press the dough with your fingertips; if they leave a stubborn imprint, it has risen enough.)

When the rising time is almost over, presoak a clay pot, top and bottom, for 15 minutes.

Roll the dough out to a thickness of ¼ inch. Place the sausages (about 5) on top of the dough, wrap each in its own pocket, and pinch the ends closed. Place each pocket side by side to form one loaf. Trim a piece of aluminum foil, cover the bottom of the bottom of the presoaked pot and sprinkle with cornmeal. Add the dough to the pot and put lid on, then put the covered pot in a warm place and let the dough rise until doubled in size (about 60 minutes).

Cover the pot and place it in a cold oven.

Set the oven temperature at 450 degrees.

Bake for 45 minutes, then check the bread and let it continue, uncovered, in the oven to brown for an additional 15 minutes (total cooking time about 60 minutes). The bread will be done when a finger thump on the loaf's surface sounds hollow.

Allow the bread to sit for 15 to 20 minutes before serving.

Note: This recipe can be safely doubled, but use 2 pots for cooking.

RYE BREAD WITH WILD SEED MIX

By now we've all gotten pretty well turned off that tasteless, mushy, air-inflated guck, packaged and preserved with who knows what, that passes for "bread." The Consumer Revolt has filled supermarket shelves with organic bread, wheatberry bread, stone-ground bread, and myriad improvements over the common loaf. But until you've tried this heavenly rye with seeds baked in the wet-pot, you'll never know why they called it "the staff of life."

2 packages active dry yeast or 1 ounce fresh yeast
¾ cup lukewarm water
¼ cup molasses
1½ tablespoons salt
3½ cups rye flour
3 tablespoons caraway seeds
1 tablespoon poppy seeds
1 tablespoon sesame seeds
1 teaspoon celery seeds
¾ cup lukewarm buttermilk
1 egg, beaten
2 tablespoons melted butter
2 cups white flour

Combine the yeast, lukewarm water, molasses, and salt. Set aside to allow the yeast to dissolve.

Combine the rye flour and all the seeds in a large mixing bowl.

In a separate bowl, combine the buttermilk, beaten egg, and

melted butter, then add to the rye flour–seed mixture. Add the yeast mixture, then add the all-purpose flour.

Knead the mixture on a floured counter or bread board, until smooth and elastic, then place the dough in a large greased bowl. Cover with a damp cloth and allow to rise in a warm place for about 2 hours, or until the dough doubles in bulk. When the rising time is about over, presoak a large clay pot, top and bottom, in water for 15 minutes.

Punch the dough down and reshape it into one round loaf. Place a small piece of aluminum foil on the bottom of the presoaked pot to prevent sticking, then place the dough in the pot, cover, and allow to rise in a warm place for about 1 hour, or until doubled in bulk.

Cover the pot and place it in a cold oven.

Set the oven temperature at 480 degrees.

Bake for 55 minutes, removing the lid for the last 5 minutes to brown the crust.

Note: You can make this into 2 small loaves, baking them in separate pots for 45 minutes.

ONION DILL BREAD

This recipe can easily be doubled, but use two pots, one for each loaf.

>1¼ cups lukewarm water
>1 teaspoon salt
>1 tablespoon chopped fresh dillweed
>Large pinch of powdered saffron
>1 package active dry yeast
>4 cups sifted all-purpose flour
>⅛ cup olive oil
>1 onion, chopped fine
>¼ green pepper, chopped fine
>1½ tablespoons butter

In a large metal bowl, combine the lukewarm water, salt, dillweed, saffron, and the yeast (crumbling it until well dissolved). Keep the metal bowl lukewarm to keep the yeast active.

Sift the flour into a large bowl and make a well in the center. Pour the yeast mixture into the well and stir, then knead the dough with your hands for about 10 minutes, or until the dough is smooth and elastic. Pour the olive oil over the dough and knead (about 5 minutes) until it is no longer sticky.

Put the dough in a large bowl, cover with a towel, and set in a warm place until the dough doubles in size. When the rising time is about over, presoak a clay pot, top and bottom, in water for 10 minutes.

Sauté the onion and green pepper in the butter until tender but not browned, then remove the pan from the heat to cool. While it is cooling, roll the dough into an oblong ¼-inch thick. Sprinkle the onion and green pepper mixture over the dough and fold in half lengthwise. Cut dough into three long strips and braid into a loaf.

Place a piece of aluminum foil in the bottom of the presoaked pot. Place the braided loaf in the pot, cover with lid, and let rise in a warm place until doubled in size (about 60 minutes).

Cover the pot and place it in a cold oven.

Set the oven temperature at 450 degrees.

Bake for 45 minutes, then remove the pot from the oven and check bread for doneness. Return the pot to the oven, uncovered, and brown for additional 15 minutes. (Bread will be done when a finger thump on the loaf's surface sounds hollow.)

Allow the bread to cool for 15 to 20 minutes before serving.

CORNISH SAFFRON CAKE

Miners from Cornwall were addicted to this golden cake. When they migrated to work the silver, gold and copper lodes of the American West, their wives took this recipe with them.

> 2 *packages active dry yeast or 1 ounce fresh yeast*
> ½ *cup lukewarm water*
> ½ *cup (1 stick) softened butter*
> 1 *teaspoon salt*
> 2 *cups sugar*
> ½ *teaspoon Spanish saffron*
> ¼ *cup boiling water*
> ¾ *cup lukewarm milk*
> 4 *cups all-purpose flour*
> ¾ *cup white raisins*
> ¾ *cup currants*
> ¾ *cup chopped almonds*

Dissolve the yeast in the lukewarm water and set aside in a warm place.

Combine the butter, salt, and sugar in a large mixing bowl.

Dissolve the saffron in the ¼ cup boiling water, then let cool; add the yeast mixture, milk, butter, sugar, and 2 cups of the flour. Beat until smooth, gradually adding the remaining 2 cups of flour. Knead to a smooth, elastic dough, place in a large greased bowl, and allow to rise until doubled in bulk. When the rising time is about over, presoak 2 medium-sized clay pots, top and bottom, in water for 15 minutes.

Punch the dough down, add the raisins, currants, and nuts, and knead into 2 large, round loaves. Cover the bottom of each presoaked pot with a small piece of aluminum foil to prevent sticking, then place one loaf in each pot, cover with lid, and allow to rise in a warm place until the dough almost doubles in size.

Cover the pots and place them in a cold oven.

Set the oven temperature at 450 degrees.

Bake for 50 minutes, or until a finger thump on the bread's surface sounds hollow.

CARROT BREAD

A rich bread, slightly sweet, suitable for Sunday brunch.

1½ packages active dry yeast or ¾ ounce fresh yeast
¼ cup lukewarm water
3½ to 4 cups all-purpose flour
⅔ teaspoon salt
1 cup granulated sugar
½ cup brown sugar
2 eggs, beaten
2 cups shredded carrots
⅓ cup cooking oil
½ cup chopped·walnuts

Dissolve the yeast in the lukewarm water and set aside.

In a large bowl, combine 3½ cups of the flour, salt and sugar. In a separate bowl, combine the beaten eggs, shredded carrots, cooking oil, and chopped nuts. Mix well and add the yeast mixture, then knead into a round ball, using the remaining ½ cup flour, if necessary.

Place the dough in a greased bowl, cover with a damp cloth, and set aside in a warm place to allow the dough to rise.

Just before rising time is over, soak 2 clay pots, tops and bottoms, in water for 15 minutes.

Punch the dough down and reshape into 2 round loaves.

Place a small piece of aluminum foil on the bottom of each presoaked pot to prevent sticking.

Place the loaves in the pots, cover with the lid and allow to rise until nearly doubled in bulk.

Place the covered pots in a cold oven.

Set the temperature at 450 degrees.

Bake about 50 minutes, until a finger thump on the bread's surface sounds hollow.

Note: You can reserve half of the dough, covered in the refrigerator, if you want to bake only one loaf. You can bake the other loaf several days later.

Desserts

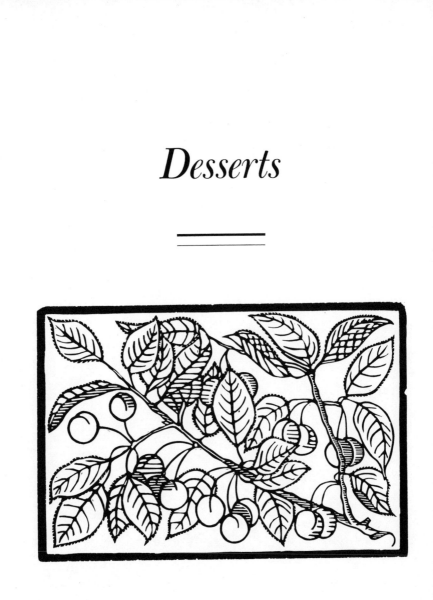

FLAMING BANANA

H E R E's the perfect topper to cut the salty-spicyness of Romertopf's Beggar's Chicken (page 12) or Lamb Curry (page 158). Be sure the bananas are on the slightly greenish side, much better for cooking, in contrast to *eating* bananas, which are not ready for consumption until the skin is liberally freckled with brown spots.

> 2 *slightly green bananas*
> 2 *tablespoons melted butter*
> 2 *tablespoons granulated sugar*
> 2 *tablespoons rum, 150 proof*
> *Whipped cream*

Presoak a clay pot, top and bottom, in water for 15 minutes.
Peel the bananas and place in the presoaked pot.
Combine the melted butter, sugar, and 1 tablespoon of the rum and add to the pot.
Cover the pot and place it in a cold oven.
Set the oven temperature at 450 degrees.
Cook for 25 minutes.
Remove the pot from the oven and prepare to serve at the table.

Warm the remaining rum in a saucepan, pour over the
bananas, and ignite. Wiggle the pot gently to prolong the
flame, then serve with whipped cream. As long as you're
not on a diet, might as well go all the way.

GEORGIA PEACH PIE

(SERVES 4)

This deep-dish pie is a natural in the wet-pot. Be sure the peaches aren't mushy-overripe, but still firm. The macaroons make a distinctive crust; get them crisp, not chewy-moist.

> 5 *large peaches (not* too *ripe)*
> ½ *cup brown sugar*
> ¾ *cup granulated sugar*
> 1 *tablespoon (1 envelope) unflavored gelatin*
> ¼ *cup finely chopped walnuts*
> ¼ *teaspoon salt*
> 10 crisp *macaroons, crumbled*
> 2 *tablespoons Kirsch*
> 2 *teaspoons butter*

Presoak a clay pot, top and bottom, in water for 15 minutes.

Peel and slice the peaches, then place them in the bottom of the presoaked pot. Combine the brown sugar, granulated sugar, gelatin, chopped nuts, and salt and pour over the peaches. Dot the top with the butter, then add the Kirsch and top with crumbled macaroons.

Cover the pot and place it in a cold oven.

Set the oven temperature at 500 degrees.

Cook for 50 minutes, or until done.

Remove the lid for the last 10 minutes to brown the crust.

POACHED PEARS

(SERVES 3)

Be sure the pears are firm, underripe. Cooking time depends upon the degree of ripeness, so test for doneness by removing from the oven after 30 minutes and pricking the pears with a toothpick; the fruit should be easily penetrated, but not too hard.

3 firm pears
Juice of ½ lemon
3 tablespoons honey
¾ cup white wine
1 cup sour cream

Presoak a clay pot, top and bottom, in water for 10 minutes.
Peel the pears and cut in half lengthwise, then place in the presoaked pot, cut side down, and sprinkle with the lemon juice. Combine the honey and white wine in a warmed bowl and pour over the pears.
Cover the pot and place it in a cold oven.
Set the oven temperature at 450 degrees.
Cook for approximately 45 minutes (depending on the degree of ripeness of the pears).
Serve with the sour cream.

Variations: Top with a purée of sweetened raspberries or apricot sauce. Just before serving, add heated Kirsch or brandy.

ITALIAN BAKED PEARS

(SERVES 4)

The mixture of pears and dark chocolate may sound odd at first, but this "easy-to-make" recipe makes a marvelous dessert.

Note: The "zest" of a lemon is the outer yellow skin scraped with a bar tool.

> 4 *firm, underripe pears*
>   (*try to get Anjous or Winter Nellis*)
> 4 *teaspoons granulated sugar*
> ¼ *cup semisweet chocolate bits*
> ¼ *teaspoon grated lemon zest*
> 1 *cup dry Marsala*
> ½ *pint whipping cream*
> ½ *teaspoon vanilla extract*

Presoak a clay pot, top and bottom, in water for 10 minutes.
Core the pears without breaking through the bottoms. Put
  1 teaspoon sugar in each pear cavity, top with some chocolate bits, and sprinkle with lemon zest. Place the pears
  in the presoaked pot and pour the Marsala into the pear
  cavities and over pears.
Cover the pot and place it in a cold oven.
Set the oven temperature at 450 degrees.
Bake for 45 to 50 minutes. (Test after 45 minutes by pricking
  the pears with a toothpick; the pears should be soft, though
  not mushy.)

Cool a metal bowl in the freezer, then whip the cream in it until slightly stiff. Add the remaining teaspoon vanilla. Continue whipping until the cream just comes to a constant peak, but is not too stiff. Top the pears with whipped cream and serve.

Note: For an added touch, sprinkle the pears and whipped cream with some good Italian macaroons.

PHILADELPHIAN BAKED APPLES

(SERVES 4)

6 *medium-sized, hard green apples*
1 *eight-ounce package cream cheese*
3 *tablespoons honey*
1½ *tablespoons finely chopped walnuts*

Presoak a clay pot, top and bottom, in water for 10 minutes.
Core the apples, removing all the seeds but being careful not
to break through the bottoms of the apples. Combine the
cream cheese, honey, and walnuts and stuff the cavities
of the apples, then place the apples in the presoaked pot.
Cover the pot and place it in a cold oven.
Set the oven temperature at 450 degrees.
Cook for 40 minutes, test by pricking with a toothpick after
30 minutes.

Variation: Top with whipped cream sweetened with sugar
and a dash of vanilla.

GRANDMA'S GREEN APPLE PIE

(SERVES 6)

This down-home recipe from Georgia's grandmother in Great Falls is more of a cobbler than a pie, but whether sliced or scooped out, it still drips with that old-fashioned flavor. The little green apples should be very hard and tart—the tarter the apple, the better the pie. It should be served with a sharp Cheddar cheese.

> 1 *dozen small, hard, tart green apples*

COMBINE:

> 1½ *cups granulated sugar*
> ¼ *cup all-purpose flour*
> ¼ *teaspoon salt*
> 1 *scant teaspoon ground cinnamon*
> *Pinch of ground cloves*
> 2 *tablespoons butter*
> *Pastry for a one-crust pie (your own or see below)*

Presoak a clay pot, top and bottom, in water for 10 minutes. Core and peel the apples, slice them thin, and place in the bottom of the presoaked pot. You should have about 5 cups of sliced apples. Combine the sugar, flour, salt, cinnamon, and cloves and pour over the apples. Stir the contents of the pot so that all the apples are coated. Cut the butter into small pieces and sprinkle over the apples.

Make the crust, roll it out, and shape it over the apples.

Cover the pot with the lid.

Place the pot in a cold oven.

Set the oven temperature at 480 degrees.

Cook for 45 minutes.

Check the pie for doneness, then remove the lid and return the pot to the oven for an additional 15 minutes to brown the crust.

Serve with a very sharp Cheddar cheese.

PIE CRUST:

> 1 *cup all-purpose flour*
> ¼ *cup shortening*
> 1 *teaspoon salt*
> 1½ *tablespoons cold water*

Mix the flour, shortening, and salt until crumbly. Add the cold water and mix lightly. Place the dough between two sheets of waxed paper and roll to the desired size.

Index

THE AUTHORS

Grover Sales, San Francisco writer, is film and drama critic for KQED, National Educational Television, and instructor of music and drama at University of California Extension.

Georgia MacLeod Sales, one of the few licensed women architects in the San Francisco Bay area, is co-owner of Architectural Interiors, a Sausalito firm specializing in commercial interior design.